PRETEEN DEVOTIONAL for GIRLS

52 WEEKS OF ENCOURAGING DEVOTIONS & SCRIPTURE FOR TWEENS

Brittany

Zeitgeist · New York

This book is dedicated to
my beautiful nieces, Lily, Pearl,
Emma, Abigail, Addison,
Lois, and Kennedy, whom I
had in my heart when I wrote
this book.

*May the Lord bring good to you
and keep you. May the Lord
make His face shine upon you,
and be kind to you. May the
Lord show favor toward you,
and give you peace.*

—NUMBERS 6:24–26 (NLV)

Contents

PART THREE

Relationships

PART FOUR
Feelings & Identity

Introduction

The preteen years can be pretty hard sometimes. But I'll let you in on a little secret: they are for *everyone*. No, really. Even if you see someone your age acting like they have it all together, I can promise you they don't.

I remember wrestling with a lot of questions: *Who am I? Where do I fit in? Who am I meant to be?* The one difference you and I might have, though, is that I didn't know anything about God when I was your age.

I didn't grow up in a home that went to church or talked about God. I felt so alone and lost until as a teenager, I went to youth group with a friend. When I heard the youth pastor share the Gospel, my whole life changed! I was far from God, a messed-up teenager, but when I gave my heart to Jesus, He made me a completely new person! And He has been with me every day, helping me to answer those questions and be the person God created me to be.

I want to encourage you right where you are: God has all those answers and more already figured out. But you'll never know the answers unless you seek Him with all your heart. That's why a book like this is so important to have by your side. I'm going to share with you what God says in His Word and give you practical steps to draw closer to Him.

You don't have to navigate this journey alone, sister. And I truly believe that on the other side of this devotional is you with a stronger relationship with God!

How to Use This Book

I remember the first time I read a devotional book. I was a teenager, only a few years older than you, and I was a new Christian. There are many types of books out there—fiction, educational, and so on—but I wasn't sure how to approach the one I held in my hands. The devotions were short and had questions not usually found in books. Let me help you avoid that awkward situation with a quick breakdown on how you can work through this book.

WHAT'S IN THIS BOOK?

This book has 52 devotions in it: one for every week of the year. It doesn't matter which day of the week you choose to study, but I would encourage you to choose the same day each week. Finding consistency and keeping a rhythm will help you make time for this book (even when you get discouraged or busy).

Each devotion will talk about something that is important to you, in a way that makes sense. But even better, each devotion will pull significant truths directly from God's Word.

At the beginning of every devotion, I'll share a Bible verse followed by some insight that will help you understand the passage better. Then, at the end, there will be a few questions to help you apply the verses to your own life and, finally, a closing prayer to God to invite Him into your growing process.

UNDERSTANDING GOD'S WORD

It takes practice, time, and a desire to hear from God, but the more time you spend reading the Bible, the more you'll learn to hear from Him. Here are some tips I've picked up that have helped me to better understand Scripture and to learn to hear from God:

- ⭐ *Read the Bible every day.* Starting the day with God's Word makes me feel more at peace and connected to Him, ready to take on the day! The Bible is the only thing that we know is definitely from God, and reading it is one of the most beneficial things you can do.
- ⭐ *Pray for understanding.* Nobody knows God's Word better than Him! Before you read the Bible, ask God to help you understand what He wants to say to you.
- ⭐ *Ask a parent, guardian, or youth leader to help you understand the meaning of the passage.* Sometimes we might read a passage and have a hard time interpreting what God means. Asking someone else can help you see something in a new light.
- ⭐ *Read devotionals or books that talk about the Bible.* There are many books written about God and the Bible. Reading them can help us learn more about Him, His Word, and different life topics.
- ⭐ *Memorize Bible verses.* There are verses I memorized almost twenty years ago that I still remember. And what's so cool is that when I'm in a difficult situation, God will remind me of that verse to encourage me!

STAYING MOTIVATED AND FOCUSED

Sometimes you'll get tired, forget, or be discouraged about reading this book. You know what? It's usually the Enemy wanting you to give up, because he knows reading books like this and the Bible is good for you. He wants you to prioritize everything else, or be tired from sports practice, or stay upset after a fight with a friend. When you lose focus or get sidetracked, here are some tips to help motivate you:

- ★ **Find a time that works best for you.** If you're reading this book when you're really tired or during a busy time in the day, you might give up more readily. Pick a time when you're most awake, free, and motivated! For me, it's first thing in the morning, before the busyness begins. For a friend of mine, it's at night because she's tired in the mornings. Maybe weekends work better for you because you have more free time. Pick a time that allows you to focus!
- ★ **Read at the same time every week.** Routine can be helpful to create habits. If you choose the same time and day each week to read this book, you're more likely to keep up with it.
- ★ **Ask God to renew your desire.** Whenever I'm feeling discouraged, I pray and ask God to help me crave His Word and presence. A simple prayer can be just the thing to excite you again!
- ★ **See if a friend wants to read the book with you.** Doing something with another person is a helpful way to keep up a habit. Ask one of your friends to read the book, and you can keep each other accountable.

PART ONE

Faith

Why Jesus?

Following God isn't always the most popular thing to do. People will tell you He isn't real, and the world will do everything it can to make Him seem anything but good. But can I share with you the best news in the world?

Jesus is real, and He is so good!

You and I live in a world that is covered in darkness—not actual darkness but an invisible one that makes this world difficult to live in. It makes people treat others unkindly, creates confusion about God, and allows bad things to happen to good people.

Have you ever been in a dark room and a cell phone light clicked on or a candle was lit? The light stands out so much more in the darkness. That's Jesus. He is this beautiful, shining light in a world of darkness. He is the warmth flickering in the cold. He is the glow that lights your steps when things get hard.

Why follow Jesus? Because He is the light, goodness, and love when everything else is imperfect and hard. Jesus can calm your storms, replace your fear with peace, and give you strength to make it through the difficult days. He gives you hope, direction, and love in a world that often tries to take all those things away.

For those who follow Jesus—making Him number one—there is life! And that means two things. First, He gives you a time on earth filled with peace and joy, even when you feel scared or things aren't easy.

Second, He gives you life after death. You see, Jesus came to earth and lived a perfect life, then died on a cross and rose again. He conquered death when He came back to life, and He did it for you! And because of that, those who follow Jesus with their whole heart get to spend forever in heaven with Him when they die.

You are very special to Jesus and He wants a relationship with you. Following Him is the best decision you can ever make, and it will give you a life so much sweeter than you can imagine!

1) Do you believe Jesus is perfect? Why or why not?
2) What about Jesus makes you feel safe and happy?
3) Have you had a hard day or week but felt better after praying or going to church? Why do you think that is?
4) Have you made a decision to follow Him with all your heart for the rest of your life?
5) If so, how does that make you feel? If not, what is holding you back?

PRAYER Jesus, thank You for loving me so much that You died for me. That's the best love in the world! And thank You for bringing light and goodness into this dark world and into my life. I want to trust You with all my heart; will You help me to do that every day? I love and want to follow You alone. Amen.

WEEK 2 You Are Loved

When I was in junior high and high school, people could buy carnations to deliver to students on Valentine's Day. It was always a surprise and made you feel special when you received one. How many you received—if you received one at all—felt like an indication of your worth.

I used to always hope I'd receive at least one carnation each year; I wanted to feel special and loved. It didn't matter if it was a friend, a crush, or my parents giving the flower—I just needed to feel loved, and I thought a flower could make me feel cared for. One year in high school, when I was on the dance team, some of my teammates sent me a flower, and I remember feeling so special!

Then I became a Christian, and I encountered a love unlike anything I had previously experienced. It didn't come in the form of a carnation; it came in the form of a sacrifice. It's an immeasurable love Jesus has not just for me, but for you too.

Did you know there is nothing you can do to make God love you any more or any less? You are so incredibly special. You know why? It's not because you look or act a certain way. It's because you are God's daughter, and you are incredibly beautiful in His sight. A parent loves their child more than anything, and that's how God feels

What marvelous love the Father has extended to us! Just look at it—we're called children of God! That's who we really are. But that's also why the world doesn't recognize us or take us seriously, because it has no idea who he is or what he's up to.

1 JOHN 3:1 (MSG)

about you. In fact, God loves you so much that He sent His only Son, Jesus, to die for you.

You know what's perhaps the best part of God's love? You don't have to earn it. God sees you right now, knowing everything about you, and He still chooses to love you! So, whatever you might feel about yourself or your worth, hold that up to God's love for you, and you'll see it doesn't compare to what He thinks of you.

1) Do you feel loved in your life? It could be by family, friends, or God.

2) What do you think about being called a "child of God"? Does this make you feel special?

3) Do you ever feel the unnecessary pressure to perform to make God love you? In what ways have you tried to earn His love before?

4) What's one thing you read in this devotion that encouraged you or made you feel better?

5) How can you, in return, show your love to God today?

PRAYER God, thank You for loving me. I'm so excited and grateful to be Your daughter, and I hope You will help me to live in that identity and from a place of Your special love. On the days I forget and don't feel very special, will You please remind me of just how much You love me? I love You too, God. You are very special to me! Amen.

WEEK 3 The Power of Prayer

You have a powerful tool in your spiritual warfare belt—prayer. Prayer changes things, and you can see this all throughout the Bible when people pray and God moves.

As a teenager, I was confused about what prayer meant and looked like, so let me share a few thoughts about it:

★ **Prayer is a conversation with God.** There is no formula to prayer, and no right or wrong way to do it. Talk to Him as you would a friend.

★ **Prayer should become a regular part of your day.** First Thessalonians 5:17 says we should pray without ceasing. That doesn't mean you're never supposed to stop; that would be impossible! It simply means you pray throughout the day, whether that be before a meal or a test, when you have a problem with a friend, or even when you're waiting for the bus. Talk to God throughout your day!

★ **Learn to pray according to His will.** The verse for this devotion says, "that if we ask anything according to his will he hears us." You can ask for a brand-new phone, but that may not happen because it may not be His will. In another situation, you might pray for a friend to heal from a sickness, and He answers that prayer because it is in His will. The more time you spend getting to know Him, the better you'll come to know His will and desires.

Prayer isn't a magic wand you wave over your troubles to make them disappear. Its primary purpose isn't to change God's mind, but to change yours. Does that make sense? Through regular conversation with God, you become more like Him. As you become more like Him, you'll begin to pray for the things He desires.

Be a prayer warrior—this world needs more of those!

1) Do you pray every day? Why or why not? What's stopping you?

2) What's one thing you learned in this devotional about prayer that you didn't already know?

3) How will you add more prayer into your daily routine?

4) Do you believe God wants to answer your prayers? Why or why not?

5) What is one prayer you have right now that you could really use God's help with?

PRAYER Oh God, I'm so glad to know that You hear my prayers. Every word I say to You makes it to Your ears, and I am heard by You, my good Father. Please help me make prayer really important in my life and learn how to pray in agreement with You and Your will. Amen!

WEEK 4 Being Like Jesus

For a long time, I wanted to be like other people. Whether it was the popular girl at school, or someone who was doing what I wanted to do one day, or simply anyone not going through what I was going through, there have been so many times I just wanted to be someone else.

But you know what? There's only one person I want to be like now: Jesus. You know why? Because He is the most amazing person to have ever lived, and if there is one person we should want to be like, it's Him.

In the Bible, you and I are called to be less like this world and more like Jesus. And how do we do that? Ephesians 5 shows us:

> Watch what God does, and then you do it, like children who learn proper behavior from their parents. Mostly what God does is love you. Keep company with him and learn a life of love. Observe how Christ loved us. His love was not cautious but extravagant. He didn't love in order to get something from us but to give everything of himself to us. Love like that.
>
> **EPHESIANS 5:1–2 (MSG)**

★ ***Watch Him and do what He did.*** Read the Bible and find out how Jesus treated people. You'll see that He valued following the Father's will, and you'll be able to learn so many wonderful things about life from Him. Things such as what it looks like to be blessed, how to find your passions, and what hope we have. As you learn about God, His desires, and His hopes, live how He lived.

★ ***Give a lot of love.*** Jesus was very concerned about others, and He always showed love to people by serving them. Love the people around you because, when you do, you're pointing them back to Jesus!

If you try to act as Jesus did, and care about the things He cared about, you will become more like Him. You'll become someone more loving, giving, kind, and patient. I don't know about you, but that's someone I always want to be like!

1) **What do you know about Jesus that makes you want to be more like Him?**

2) **What is one thing you can do this week that would follow the model of Jesus' life?**

3) **Who can you show love to today and how?**

4) **What is one thing you know about Jesus that you really love about Him?**

5) **Is there an area in your life where you're struggling to be like Jesus? Maybe at home or at school? How can you be more like Jesus there?**

PRAYER Jesus, You are so good and loving. Thank You for being both to me! You are so special to me, and I really do look up to You. Please help me to be more like You. Help me to let go of the things that are more like this world and become the girl You created me to be. Amen.

WEEK 5 Standing Firm in Your Faith

So, my dear brothers and sisters, be strong and immovable. Always work enthusiastically for the Lord, for you know that nothing you do for the Lord is ever useless.

1 CORINTHIANS 15:58 (NLT)

The world can be tough. When life gets too hard or someone pressures you to do something that isn't right, you might even think about trying the world's way of living and give up on God.

When I was in junior high, I didn't have a lot of material things. I thought that having better clothes or makeup would make me feel better about myself, so once I stole a shirt from a store in my local mall. I felt so anxious during and after the theft because I knew what I was doing was wrong. On top of that, I didn't feel better about myself at all. Clothes couldn't fix what was broken in me—only Jesus could!

But I want to encourage you to stay strong! You see, I have given up doing things the right way or given in to things I knew were wrong. And guess what? I regret every single time I did something I felt or knew wasn't right. Why? Because it has always left me feeling empty and sad. I don't want that for you—you are meant for something truly wonderful in the Kingdom of God!

Will you try to stay firm in your belief in God? Will you give your best to Him, following Him wholeheartedly? When you feel something is wrong, run from the temptation. When someone at school pressures you to lie, steal, or bully, stand as an example for what's good. Be strong and immovable!

Live fully for God and do the things you know He asks you to do in the Bible. Things like being kind, being in a community with like-minded friends, and honoring your parents. When you do these things, God sees them and remembers your faithfulness. Nothing you do for God is useless, and you will be rewarded for your steadfast belief in Him.

1) Do you sometimes feel like it's hard to be a Christian? Why is that?

2) Have you ever done something you regretted? How does it make you feel to know God forgives every sin if you'll only ask Him to forgive you?

3) Is there something or someone tempting you to compromise? How are you going to respond and do the right thing?

4) Are there things you can do to strengthen your faith, like going to youth group or reading your Bible more?

5) What excites you about knowing God honors your faithfulness?

PRAYER God, You are so good, and I want to honor You with my life. I want to give You my all and stand firm in my faith even though life is hard. Will You please help me to be a strong Christian and make the right choices? I want to be more like You and be an example for others of how good You are. Amen.

WEEK 6 Sharing Your Faith

You and I have one important mission in this life—to tell people about Jesus! That's why we're all still here and not in heaven. It's because God wants us to go and tell as many people about Him so that others might know Him too.

Sometimes it can be hard talking to people about God. You might be afraid of what others will think. Perhaps you're not sure what to say. I've been there! I too have worried that people might reject me or that I wouldn't say the right thing. But consider this: if you don't tell them about Jesus, maybe nobody ever will. You could be the person whom God wants to use to make Himself known. Here are a few things to consider.

First, you don't have to have the perfect words or know everything about the Bible to lead someone to Jesus. All you have to do is tell someone how good God is and how He has been good to you. Tell people how God has helped you.

Second, they might not want to give their life to Jesus, and that's not on you. God works in mysterious ways. He can use you to make a connection, and one day, when they are ready, this person can grow through Him. Help change a person's life by planting a seed today that, down the road, God will water.

But most of all, live out how much you love Jesus and how happy He makes you. Actions usually speak louder than words. When you live by example, you point others around you to Jesus and show them that they too have His love.

1) What scares you most about telling others about Jesus, and why?
2) Write out your own testimony, why you love God, and how He has been good to you.
3) Who is one person you can tell about Jesus this week?
4) What will you say to that person? Write it out and practice speaking out loud to get more comfortable.
5) How can you live out your faith? This can be done by being nice to someone who other people aren't nice to or by helping a neighbor.

PRAYER Jesus, thank You for Your love and grace, and for saving me and loving me so much. I want others to know that grace and love too. Please help me not to be afraid to tell people about You. I want to be a witness, and I ask that You please help me to do that well. In Jesus' name I pray. Amen.

Why Go to Church?

I love going to church. In fact, it's the closest place to home for me. When I first became a Christian as a teenager, I attended my church as much as possible. It was a safe space for me. I met wonderful people, learned about God, and grew in maturity. Even today, it's a favorite place of mine.

God lives in fellowship within the Father, the Son, and the Holy Spirit, and it's His desire for you and me to live in fellowship too—both with Him and with others. At church, we get both. We get to spend time in His sweet presence and with other Christians.

If you're wondering why you should attend church, here are a few things to consider:

★ **Community is good for us.** Who you spend time with is one of the biggest influences on the person you become. That's why you want to surround yourself with Christian friends, and what better place to find them than at church? Plus, as the verse above mentions, coming together at church is how we help our friends.

★ **We get to worship God in a group.** The verse mentions that we should not give up worshipping together. It will feel encouraging to worship with other people who love God. It's a sweet reflection of what heaven will be like!

★ ***We can learn a lot at church.*** We can learn about God and what He wants for us, as well as learn a lot about ourselves. When you attend a Bible-believing church and hear from a pastor who teaches God's Word rightly, it is so encouraging to your faith! Hearing from Bible teachers helps us to grow in our understanding of God's Word.

I loved going to youth group as a teenager. I met many great friends there, learned about God, and discovered my passions. I hope, if you don't already, that you'll also learn to love church. Try to go, even when you don't feel like it or you're busy.

1) Do you go to church every week? Why or why not?

2) Who are your friends at church, and how can you all grow together as believers?

3) Is there someone you can bring to church with you?

4) What obstacles keep you from going to church? These could be hobbies, or simply not having a ride.

5) How can you remove those obstacles?

PRAYER Jesus, I know You love the Church so much. Please help me to make it really important to go every week, even when I don't feel like it or there's something else to do. I want to be in a place that helps me grow and become more like You. Also, please help me to invite others to go with me. Amen.

PART TWO

Character

What Does God Want?

Sometimes it can be a lot to think about all the things we should and shouldn't do. If you ever feel that way, start with these Bible verses, which contain the two most important things you should do:

1) **Love God as much as you can.**
2) **Then love others.**

Loving God is the greatest commandment and what you should achieve before anything else. Because when you love God that much, you will want to do other important things, such as reading the Bible, following His teachings, and being more like Him. From that place of love will flow obedience and trust.

God loves you more than anyone could ever love you. He loves you so much that Jesus died for you. What He really wants is to have a relationship with you, where you love Him back. Nobody could ever love God as much as He loves us, but we can sure try loving Him as much as possible.

So, if life seems hard and too much to work through, start with loving God. Matthew 6:33 says that, when you put God first, all the other important things in your life will be taken care of.

From that place of loving God, learn to love others. How you treat people speaks volumes about the kind of person you are. I pray that your life says you care about others, because God really cares about them too. He even says in the Bible that how you treat the least of these—which can mean anyone you come across—is how you treat God (Matthew 25:40). What you do for others truly does represent your love for God.

1) What is one thing you learned today that was helpful?
2) How can you show God today how much you love Him?
3) How has God shown you that He loves you?
4) In what way would you like to be more like Jesus?
5) Is there someone you can show love to today?

PRAYER God, thank You for loving me so much. I know I can never love You more than You love me, but I want to try. I want to love You more and more each day. Please take out of my life the things that keep me back from giving You my all. And help me to love others. Amen.

Kindness Is Beautiful

Kind words are like honey—sweet to the soul and healthy for the body.

PROVERBS 16:24 (NLT)

Kindness is a beautiful thing to witness in a person. Kind individuals are the ones other good people are drawn to.

In middle school and high school, I knew a girl a year younger than me, named Elisha. She was so nice and genuine. Everyone really liked her. She was popular and never unkind to a soul, which drew everyone to her. It didn't matter who you were—Elisha treated everyone as a friend.

Elisha was also a Christian. And not just someone who said she was but never acted on it. No, she was someone who genuinely loved God and loved others. She was, and is, the real deal. To this day, I can still remember her standing out as a teen role model, and that is the impact and power of kindness.

It's no secret that there is a lot of pain and hurt in this world. People are cruel to those who are different from them, and a lot of hate circulates around us, which is why kindness is so needed.

Imagine what your kindness can do for others. Proverbs says that your kind words can be something really good for another person's heart. You never know—one nice word to someone can totally change their day!

In a world where people are hurting, show them kindness. Showing love could be the very thing that changes someone's day or even their life. And you know what? Kindness is one of the best ways to lead people to Jesus. They will see Him in you and want to know more.

1) Share a time when someone was kind to you and how it made you feel.

2) Talk about a Christian you know who is kind. What do you, and others, think about that person?

3) Who can you show kindness this week, and how?

4) How can you be better about showing your family and friends more kindness?

5) Is there anything that makes it hard to be kind sometimes? Like anger, shyness, or jealousy? Identify these obstacles and start asking God to help you in those areas.

PRAYER Jesus, You have been so kind to me, and I thank You for that. It has changed my life! I want to be like You and show kindness to others too. Will You please help me be a kind person and show others goodness? Even when I don't feel like it, will You give me the ability to be kind? And in that kindness, I pray others would see You in me. Amen.

Doing Good

> *The one who blesses others is abundantly blessed; those who help others are helped.*
>
> **PROVERBS 11:25 (MSG)**

It always feels good to receive a gift, doesn't it? Or when someone does something nice for you, it's a good feeling, right?

It can also feel really good to do nice things or give gifts to other people. Generosity is that great!

But there's more to giving than receiving. The Bible promises that when you bless others, you will be blessed. In fact, many verses in Scripture talk about how God blesses and gives back to those who are generous.

So many times, people have been good to me. Twice, people gave me support to be in a Bible program when I didn't have any money to continue the school year. Once, a couple paid to have my car fixed when I was broke. I've had people help me with meals, prayers, and support during really hard times. The help meant so much to me and was life-changing.

And you know what? God saw their generosity and no doubt blessed them in return for their kindness. It may not have been extra money in their bank account the next day, but the blessing was credited to them. Someway, somehow, whether on earth or in heaven, there is a blessing added to them for helping others.

Jesus tells us not to store up our treasures on earth but in heaven (Matthew 6:19-21). In these verses, God tells us to use what we have to do things that matter, like helping others and giving to your church and missions, instead of spending what you have on yourself. Where you spend your time and money tells a lot about the kind of person you are.

Use what God gives you to help others, in whatever way you can. As you do, God will remember your generosity.

1) Has someone been generous to you? Did it mean a lot to you? What was that like?

2) What has God given you to help others with? It could be time to babysit or the ability to help a neighbor with their yard. Think of something you can do to help people.

3) Who is one person you will help this week?

4) How can you help your family right now?

5) What do you see when you think of a generous person?

PRAYER Father, You are a generous God, and I'm so thankful for Your goodness toward me. I don't want to keep any goodness for myself but instead want to share that goodness with others. Help me to see how I can be generous to the people around me and live in a way that blesses others. Amen.

WEEK 11 Having a Thankful Heart

Give thanks in everything; for this is God's will for you in Christ Jesus.

1 THESSALONIANS 5:18 (CSB)

An essential part of being a Christian is having a thankful heart. As we see, it's God's will that we all be thankful.

In difficult times, it might not seem easy to be grateful. I get it—there have been times in my life when I didn't want to be thankful. Maybe sometimes you feel like that too, but there is a secret power in thanksgiving—it changes our hearts.

There is a story in the Bible about a man named David who was the best king Israel ever had. But he made mistakes, like all of us. He did a few bad things that eventually led to losing his new baby. While his child was sick, he fasted and prayed for healing. But when David found out his baby had died, he got up and praised God.

Why would someone do that? Well, it's because he loved God more than anything and anyone and believed deep down in his heart that God was good. David knew that God had other plans for him that He would use for good. So, he gave God thanks for His love and goodness.

Life won't always be easy, but there's always something to be thankful for: God! He loves you and cares for you, and He can use every hard thing for good.

One of the greatest things you can learn as a Christian is to be a thankful person. No matter what is happening in your life, you can be thankful for health, the people around you, and living in a warm house. And when people see your thankfulness, they just might want to know more about God.

1) What are three things you can be thankful for today?
2) Write down what you love about God.
3) Think of someone you know who often gives God thanks. Who is that person, and what can you learn from them?
4) Write down the verse from this week and put it somewhere you will see it. Try to remember to pray this verse every day and take time to thank God for what He's done for you.
5) Think of someone you can tell today about how grateful you are for God. Write down what you'd like to say.

PRAYER God, thank You! Thank You for loving me, taking care of me, and doing good things in my life. You are truly a great God! Will You please remind me to give You thanks in little moments or when life is hard? Help me to become a grateful person. Amen.

WEEK 12 Finding Freedom

Sometimes people have a hard time wanting to follow God because they see a list of rules in the Bible, and they don't like to be told what to do. It's like when your parents or guardian tell you to get off the phone or clean your room. We don't like doing some things (especially when we're told to do them), and there are some things we want to do that we shouldn't.

God knows what's good for you and what will hurt you. He has rules, or laws, in place so that we can live the best life possible and become more like Him. I think of them as boundaries that keep out the bad so we can flourish in the good!

In 1 John 2, God tells us that the world makes it really hard to love God and live a pure life. The world wants you to do things that are wrong to put space between you and God—the more things you do that break His heart, the more you will be pulled away from Him.

But we are also told in this passage that those who listen to and obey God find freedom from sin and get to live eternally with God in heaven. These boundaries protect you and, while they may seem

Practically everything that goes on in the world—wanting your own way, wanting everything for yourself, wanting to appear important—has nothing to do with the Father. It just isolates you from him. The world and all its wanting, wanting, wanting is on the way out—but whoever does what God wants is set for eternity.

1 JOHN 2:15–17 (MSG)

inconvenient at times, they will foster a way of living that is holy and free.

Instead of looking at the Bible and your relationship with God as a list of dos and don'ts, see them as privileges to live in freedom and joy forever with God.

1) Do you think of the Bible only as a list of rules? Why?
2) Has there been a time you did something you shouldn't have? What happened, and how did it go wrong?
3) How would you do that differently in the future?
4) What is something God asks of you that you will do this week? It could be giving money to the church or donating some of your things to someone in need or being nice to someone at school.
5) Do you believe that God loves you and only wants the best for you? Explain your answer.

PRAYER Jesus, there are times when I don't want to do something I know I should do or I don't do something I know I should. I'm sorry for when I have made bad decisions in the past. Will You please help me to make good choices in the future? I want to follow You and be obedient to Your Word. Thank You for Your strength, Lord. Amen.

A Heart for God

My child, may you give your heart to me, and may your eyes delight in my ways.

PROVERBS 23:26 (LEB)

God created people so we could be His friend. And that includes you. God wants you to be close to Him. That's what it means to give your heart to Jesus. It means you want to know Him and follow Him every day of your life and that you'll put Him before everything else.

Remember King David? Do you know why God chose him to be king? David was a young shepherd boy with no idea that he would one day rule the country. He took care of sheep for his dad, but God chose David out of everyone because David was a "man after his own heart" (1 Samuel 13:14). Meaning, David gave his whole heart to God, and because of that, God called on him to do great things. It didn't matter what he looked like or how many people liked him—it was all about his heart for God!

Have you truly decided to follow Jesus and love God every day? To give Him your heart and delight in His ways? If not, today is the day! Don't waste another minute being without His love and care and being without loving Him in return. We have no idea when our time on earth is up, but He does, and it will be too late to change our minds and give our hearts to Him. Besides, having a friendship with God is the most amazing thing ever!

1) Have you decided to give God your heart and to follow Him? If so, in what ways has your life changed?

2) If not, would you be willing to make that decision today? Say this prayer with me: *God, I think You're amazing, and I want to give my heart to You. I'm so sorry when I've messed up or done something that would hurt You. Will You please forgive me? I give You my heart and choose to follow You. Amen.*

3) If you're still not sure, what's holding you back?

4) What are some of your favorite things about God?

5) How do you think God sees you, His daughter?

PRAYER Lord, You are amazing, wonderful, and truly incredible. I want to spend the rest of my life getting to know You. You have my heart, and I choose to follow You. Thank You for loving me so much and thinking I am special. Amen.

Who Am I?

Life can be hard when you're trying to figure out your identity. It also doesn't help that your peers and influencers on TV and on social media try to tell you who they think you should be. It's all a bit confusing, isn't it?

Yet this is an important time in your life. You get to choose who you want to be, and who you are now will determine a great deal about your life later.

God knows what is best for you. So, instead of asking yourself what kind of person you want to be, try focusing on the kind of person God wants you to be. And the great news is that you don't have to search far—there are answers in the Bible!

While there are many verses that reveal God's will, verse Micah 6:8 shows us a few examples of the kind of person He wants you to be:

★ *Fair and just.* Do what is right and treat all people fairly. This leads to great character.

★ *Kind and loving.* People can be mean to each other, but you always have the free will to be kind and stand out as someone who treats others well. Be nice to the person who others aren't

> *But he's already made it plain how to live, what to do, what God is looking for in men and women. It's quite simple: Do what is fair and just to your neighbor, be compassionate and loyal in your love, and don't take yourself too seriously—take God seriously.*
>
> **MICAH 6:8 (MSG)**

nice to. Show everyone kindness, even if they don't show it to you.

★ *Humbly walking with Him.* Put God first and think of others. This is huge in what God wants from His children.

Start here, and allow God to fashion you into a beautiful person of God who reflects the love and care He gives to all.

1) Of the three—fairness, kindness, humility—which do you struggle with most, and why?

2) Have you treated someone unfairly? If so, how can you make it right with them?

3) Do you think you are kind toward others? How might you be more kind?

4) How can you put God first in your life?

5) Write down the kind of person you'd like to be.

PRAYER God, I think You're amazing, and I want to be more like You. Please help me to be less like the world and more like You. Help me to be fair, kind, and humble. Even when it's hard or I don't want to, please help me to do the right thing. Amen.

What's the Big Deal with Sin?

> It's your sins that have cut you off from God. Because of your sins, he has turned away and will not listen anymore.
>
> **ISAIAH 59:2 (NLT)**

What's the big deal about sin anyway? People all around the world do whatever they want and seem happy, don't they? Perhaps you're thinking, *Can't I do what I want and still have a good life?*

I get why you would think that. I mean, the Enemy, and the world, wants you to think life can be fun without God. But it comes with a big price.

God can't be evil—it's impossible. And evil can't be around Him either. That's why sin is so dangerous—it keeps us from God. But guess what? God created a way for us to be with Him even though we sin. Jesus came to earth, took all of our sins on Him, died, and rose again. Which means, when you decide to follow Jesus, you get to connect to God through Jesus. How amazing is that?

But it also doesn't mean it's okay to keep sinning just because Jesus will forgive you. If you love someone, you wouldn't do specific things you know would hurt that person. The same is applied to God. Sinning is hurtful.

Looking back to when I was your age, I'm sorry for a lot of things I did and wish I could take them back. I was disrespectful to my parents, and I was sometimes mean to other kids because I wanted to be cool. Even though I know Jesus forgives me, I still feel remorse.

Be really smart about how you live your life—it matters a lot—and do your best to live a life that God would be proud of.

Remember: it's not about a list of rules of what you can't do, but about how God has created a way that you can live in freedom!

1) How would you define sin? What are your thoughts about it?

2) What do you know about sin from the Bible? What are some of God's thoughts about it?

3) What are some things you know you shouldn't do?

4) Is there something you feel sorry about and don't want to do again?

5) How does it make you feel that Jesus died and took all your sins so that you could live with God forever?

PRAYER God, I know there are things in this world that hurt Your heart, and I don't want to do those things. But I also know that I can't be perfect, and I will struggle to do the right thing all the time. Please help me to do what honors You and to stay away from sin. And Jesus, I want to thank You for making a way for me. I love You so much! Amen.

WEEK 16 When You Mess Up

But if we confess our sins to him, he is faithful and just to forgive us our sins and to cleanse us from all wickedness.

1 JOHN 1:9 (NLT)

We're human, and we're all going to mess up at one point or another. It shouldn't be an excuse, but it's going to happen. So, when it does, what do you do?

Well, remember that Jesus died for us in order to take away all our sins. So, when we do something wrong, we should go to Him. First John tells us we should confess our sins to Him.

Some might think this just happens when we give our heart to Jesus and are saved, but it should be something we do every time we mess up. One of the most important things you can do in life is learn repentance—telling God what you did wrong and that you're sorry and turning away from it. Meaning, you'll try not to do it again.

Get into this mindset and practice repentance. Even thoughts can carry the weight of sin. Every time you act disrespectfully to your parents or act mean and hurt other people's feelings, repent. Tell Jesus you're sorry, ask Him to forgive you, then pray that He will give you the strength to do better next time.

Learn to apologize by approaching someone you hurt and saying you're sorry. Apologizing can seem hard. Maybe you're not sure how the other person will respond, and no one enjoys confrontation and stress. Try to set your fears aside and focus on the apology. Here are some things you can try: Pray first and ask God to help you with the right words. Pray that the person's heart will be open to you, and then go to that person and say you're sorry. Be sure to say why you're sorry—it's important to show genuine regard for their feelings and true sorrow for hurting them. Tell them how much you care about them and ask if they will forgive you. It might be a bit scary, but more often than not, the person will forgive you and it will make the relationship so much better.

You're not going to be perfect, but Jesus has made a way for you to be forgiven and cleansed from your sin if you'll repent to Him. Isn't He amazing?

1) Is there something you're sorry for that you need to talk to God about? Write down what it is and write a prayer that asks God to forgive you.

2) Think of someone you hurt this week or in the recent past. How would you apologize and ask for forgiveness? Write it down.

3) Is there a sinful habit you've developed that you want God to help you with? It could be how you treat some people, thoughts you have, or gossiping at school.

4) What obstacles prevent you from developing the good habit of repenting?

PRAYER Father, I want to thank You for making a way to be right with You when I sin. I'm not perfect, and although I will try to follow You with all my heart, I know I will mess up. Thank You, Jesus, for Your sacrifice so that I can be made right, through You. Please help me, God, , to remember to repent when I sin. Amen.

WEEK 17 My Plan vs. God's Plan

Do not fear, for I am with you; do not be afraid, for I am your God. I will strengthen you; I will help you; I will hold on to you with my righteous right hand.

ISAIAH 41:10 (CSB)

When I was in fifth grade, I tried out for the junior high cheerleading squad. I wanted it so badly because I thought it would make school a little easier for me. Maybe I'd be a bit cooler, and more people would like me. So, I got contacts right before the tryouts and gave it my all (even though I had never tumbled or cheered before).

I was devastated when I didn't make the team. I was convinced junior high wasn't going to be a good experience for me. But you know what? I'm glad I didn't make the team, because it allowed me to focus on my dancing, which paid off. I was the only freshman to make the dance team in high school! If I had cheered in junior high, I wouldn't have had the time to dance and may not have made the team in high school, which was so fun for me.

I share this with you because sometimes you are going to really want something, and it won't work out like you hoped it would. Maybe this has already happened to you. How do you react when things don't work out the way you want them to? How do you fight discouragement?

The answer is God—He alone can carry those disappointments in life. And that means trusting in Him.

In today's Bible passage, God is telling Isaiah that he doesn't have to be afraid or worried because God will take care of him, even when it's hard. It's a promise for you too!

God wants you to know that He will take care of you, even when things don't work out. In fact, when something doesn't work out the way you want, it's probably because God has something better planned for you.

Will you trust Him to provide for you, and will you trust that He knows what is best for you?

When you are upset or sad, turn to Jesus. He wants to take care of you and show you that He has the best in store for you!

1) **Have you ever wanted something, and it didn't work out? What happened?**

2) **Were you able to see how it was actually better for you that it didn't work out?**

3) **Is there something you are hoping for right now? What is it?**

4) **Do you believe that God is good and will use whatever happens for good, even if it doesn't work out the way you'd like?**

5) **Ask your parent or guardian to tell you about a time when something they wanted didn't work out and how it was actually good that it didn't. What happened there?**

PRAYER God, I know things won't work out the way I always want. Will You please help me to trust You and believe that You know what's best for me? I put my hope and faith in You alone, my God. Amen.

Your Words Matter

There is one whose foolish words cut like a sword, but the tongue of the wise brings healing. Lips that tell the truth will last forever, but a lying tongue lasts only for a little while.

PROVERBS 12:18-19 (NLV)

Has anyone ever said something to you that cut deeply? Or shared words that made you feel so good? Words are one of the most powerful things in this world! They can tear down and wreck people or build them up in encouragement.

When I was in elementary school, I wore glasses. To this day, I remember it always hurt when people called me "four-eyes" or when a boy on the bus picked on me. It made me feel like I had no value. Has something like that ever happened to you?

If you thought about it for a bit, you would probably see just how important words are to you. The words you share are powerful. The thing is, we don't always pay much attention to our words, and it can be really hard to filter our language. Even the Bible talks about how hard it is to tame the tongue (James 3:1-12).

But just because it's hard doesn't mean we shouldn't try. Your words matter! What you say to the people around you can either tear them down or build them up. The question you must ask yourself is, which would you prefer, if it were the other way around?

Use your words to encourage and inspire people, to make them feel loved and cared for, and to speak encouragement into situations that seem hard. God wants to use you and your words to bring life. So, please, choose your words carefully. It can make a huge difference in this world!

1) Has there been a time someone used words to hurt you? How did that feel?

2) Now, has someone ever said something to you that made your day? How did that feel?

3) Which way do you choose to use your words moving forward?

4) Are there certain people you realize you don't always talk kindly to? Why might it be hard to speak well to them?

5) How can you work on choosing better words moving forward?

PRAYER Jesus, I understand that words matter, and I really want to be someone who uses their words for good. Please help me to think about what I say and to choose carefully how I speak to other people. I want to share kind and thoughtful words, not uncaring or hurtful ones. Please help me, Lord, to guard my mouth and what I say for Your glory. Amen.

When No One Is Looking

Honesty guides good people; dishonesty destroys treacherous people.

PROVERBS 11:3 (NLT)

Integrity means being honest and doing what is right. Having integrity takes personal strength; it's not easy for a lot of people. But, as someone who loves God, it is one of the most important things you can learn.

Acting on something that you know isn't right, especially when no one is looking, can lead someone down a complicated path. This is how sinning works. It could start out as something as little and seemingly insignificant as gossiping and then snowball into something bigger like lying to a parent or cheating on a test.

Proverbs tells us that honesty guides good people, which means that when you choose to be led by good choices and follow God's Word, you are on a good path.

God wants His children—and that includes you—to be honest, good, and trustworthy. To be the kind of people who will treat others well. To do the right thing even when no one is looking. The thing is, God already sees and knows everything. That might sound alarming, but I see it from the perspective that God knows exactly what you are feeling and thinking, and that means He understands you and loves you.

Choose to be the kind of person who does the right thing and is led to honor God in all you do.

1) What kind of person are you when people are looking? What kind of person are you when no one is looking?

2) What hurt or emptiness are you trying to fill when you have the urge to not honor the person God knows you have the potential to be?

3) How can you make it a habit to do right by God on a daily basis, whether someone is looking or no one is looking?

4) Is there someone you admire for being a good person? Who is that person and why do you look up to them?

PRAYER Father, I know being a person of integrity is important to You, and I want to be that kind of person. Will You please help me to be honest and do what is right, even when no one is looking? I need Your help. Amen.

WEEK 20 Trusting God with All Your Heart

It's hard for me to say this, but you probably already know it. The sad truth is, people will hurt you and things won't go the way you had hoped. And sometimes, if we're not careful, we can let those hard things get in the way of trusting God with all our heart.

When I became a Christian, trust wasn't easy for me. I had been let down by people in my life, which made trusting God very difficult. But I have learned over the years that God can be trusted.

Did you know it's impossible for God to be bad or do the wrong thing? The Bible says He is good and that He does not change (James 1:17). God can only do what is good for you! And He can use all the hard things in your life for something good. It's a fact!

God will be there for you, but He wants you to trust Him, to believe that He is Who He says He is. Have faith that says, "I can't see everything, and I don't have all the answers, but I know my God

> Trust God from the bottom of your heart; don't try to figure out everything on your own. Listen for God's voice in everything you do, everywhere you go; he's the one who will keep you on track. Don't assume that you know it all. Run to God! Run from evil! Your body will glow with health, your very bones will vibrate with life! Honor God with everything you own; give him the first and the best.
>
> **PROVERBS 3:5–10 (MSG)**

does, and I will trust Him!" From the very bottom of your heart, trust Him. Even in the bad and the hard, believe He is good.

Honor God with your life by going to Him first, always. By asking for His help, believing He is good, and knowing He can do good with the hard things in your life, you will never be disappointed for trusting Him. Life may never be exactly how you want it to be, but He always does what's best for you.

1) **Are you not trusting God for something you really want or need?**

2) **Why do you think you're having a hard time trusting Him?**

3) **Do you believe God is always good? Why or why not?**

4) **How have you seen Him work good in your life?**

5) **What is one thing you can start doing to remind yourself to trust God? This could be a prayer you say every morning or a Bible verse you put on your mirror.**

PRAYER God, I know I can trust You with all my heart and that You will always do what's best for me. Even when it's hard to see, I know that You are doing good in my life. Will You please forgive me for going to other people first, rather than trusting You? I'm so sorry, God. I will try to go to You first and put all my trust in You. Amen.

WEEK 21 Becoming a Teen

As you go through puberty, you will experience a lot of change and transition. Your body is developing. This can be an exciting time but also one filled with confusion and questions. You might also feel a little afraid or alone as you go through puberty. But don't forget, your period and other new developments happening with your body happen to all girls, including those you know—girls at school, in your neighborhood, and at church. You are not alone. Everything you are experiencing is totally normal.

God designed puberty, and since He is good, this transition is too. Talk to Him about your fears and concerns. God wants to walk through everything with you. He is the perfect Counselor for every season of your life!

You can also talk to a female grown-up you trust and who has your best interest in mind. They can help you navigate the changes you're going through and help you understand the reasons for these changes.

With puberty will come the ability to mature and learn more, allowing you to flourish in life! You don't have to be afraid, because you are designed by God and every part of you is beautiful and the way you're supposed to be.

1) What changes are you going through right now?

2) Does any part scare you or make you feel weird?

3) Is there a woman who has experienced these changes who you can talk to about it? Who?

4) What kind of questions do you have for her, and what do you want to know more about?

5) Do you trust God and His plan? Share below your prayers to Him about this season of change.

PRAYER Oh God, I know there's a lot of change taking place in this season of my life. It's a lot to take in, and at times, it makes me feel afraid and alone. But I know You made my body to go through these changes, and I trust Your design. Help me to feel safe in You and find comfort, even with all that is going on in my body. Will You help me to become the woman of God You created me to be? I thank You for Your care and design. Amen.

PART THREE
Relationships

WEEK 22 The Gift of a Mentor

Remember your leaders who taught you the word of God. Think of all the good that has come from their lives, and follow the example of their faith.

HEBREWS 13:7 (NLT)

I didn't grow up in a Christian home. So, when I gave my heart to Jesus at sixteen years old, I had so much to learn about the Bible and what it looked like to be a godly woman.

In my late teens and early twenties, God sent a lot of amazing women into my life to mentor me. My pastor's wife took me under her wing and taught me about being a godly woman and leader. My youth pastor's wife showed me what it looked like to have a healthy family and be a wife and mom. My other youth pastor's wife mentored me in growing as a Christian. They helped me so much. I wouldn't be the woman I am today without them.

God cares about our growth, and He sends mentors into our lives to help us. Mentors are someone who isn't a parent. They provide an example of what it looks like to love and honor God.

Find mentors in your life, both now and as you grow up. Because we're always growing and learning, we need mentors no matter how old we are! Even now, in my thirties, I have mentors.

Start thinking about an older teen or woman who can mentor you—it could be a youth leader or a pastor's wife. Ask if you can spend some time with them before or after church. It can be intimidating asking for someone's time and attention, but most people who are already doing community work are open to mentoring. Verses in the Bible can be found that actually instruct women to mentor girls younger than them, so don't be afraid to ask!

When you do find one or two mentors, watch how they love God, treat people, and live out their faith. Be open to learning from them and growing as much as you can!

1) Name a few women or girls you would like to learn from. Who do you look up to?

2) How are you going to ask them to mentor you?

3) Run these names by a parent or guardian and write down their thoughts.

4) What are some things you would like to learn from a mentor?

5) After you have been mentored for some time, write down the major lessons you learned.

PRAYER God, I know I have a great deal to learn, and I'd like to have someone help guide me as I do. Will You please lead me to a godly mentor and give me the courage to ask them for their guidance? And when I have found one, help me to learn as much as I can about being godly. I trust Your leadership, God. Amen.

Respecting Your Parents

> Children, obey your parents in the Lord, for this is right. "Honor your father and mother" (this is the first commandment with a promise), "that it may go well with you and that you may live long in the land."
>
> **EPHESIANS 6:1–3 (ESV)**

As a preteen and teenager, I was often disrespectful to my parents, and it showed in the kind of relationship I had with them. We weren't close and didn't talk about a lot of stuff, which left me feeling pretty lonely sometimes. I fought with them and said things that hurt them. Sometimes they said things that hurt me too. Because that is how it was then, it can sometimes be like that with them today—distant and lonely. But we are working on improving our relationship, and I'm trying to honor them well.

God wants your obedience, always, and it really matters to God that children listen to and obey their parents, who are the ultimate authorities in a child's life besides God Himself. During the preteen years, as hormones are changing and emotions are overwhelming, it's easy to fall into the trap of disrespecting your parents. But God has put them in your life to help guide you and lead you to Him, and it's important you listen to them.

God says that when you do, it will go well with you. Now, what does that mean? He's saying that someone who learns to listen to and obey their parents and the authorities in their life can learn so much. Think about how much you'll miss learning and growing if you're blocking everyone out.

Sometimes you might not feel like doing what your parents ask. Or their advice goes against what you want. If this is you, try to remember that your parents love you more than anything or anyone else on earth and only want to help you to be the best you can be.

My son likes to fight me on everything. Does it make me sad to have to punish him sometimes? Yes, so much! But I do it because I love him. And that's how God is with us. Hebrews 12:6 tells us, "For the Lord disciplines the one he loves" (ESV).

God only corrects us because He loves us so much. He wants us to learn and grow, and it's the same for your parents. Honor them by listening and obeying.

1) Do you have a hard time listening to your parents? Why do you think that is?

2) Describe a time that you didn't listen to your parents. How did it make you feel afterward?

3) How do you think it made your parents feel?

4) What can you do to curb these feelings? Come up with a phrase or verse or action that you will say or do to keep from being disrespectful and disobeying.

5) Write out what you love and appreciate about your parents.

PRAYER God, I know You have given me my parents to help me learn and grow, and I'm really thankful for them. I do love them and want to honor them. Please help me to listen and obey, even when I don't want to. And when I do mess up, give me the humility to apologize and make it right. I want to honor You and them. Amen.

Should You Talk to Your Parents?

God used Moses to lead the people of Israel out of slavery, and after he had led them out, Moses began to govern. But something wasn't quite right, and it was Moses' father-in-law, Jethro, who noticed.

You see, Moses was trying to lead and advise thousands of people all by himself. Seems like a big job, doesn't it? And Jethro could tell it was too much for Moses and it wasn't helping the people in the best way.

So, he gave Moses some wisdom to keep him from burning out and hurting the people.

Your parents can help you with hard stuff in your life. Maybe you're having a rough time with your homework and grades. Share that with your parents or guardian so that they can help you get back on track. Or maybe someone at school is being mean to you. Talk to your parents about it and they can help you handle the situation in a godly way.

Moses said to his father-in-law, "Because the people come to me with questions about God. When something comes up, they come to me. I judge between a man and his neighbor and teach them God's laws and instructions." Moses' father-in-law said, "This is no way to go about it. You'll burn out, and the people right along with you. This is way too much for you—you can't do this alone. Now listen to me. Let me tell you how to do this so that God will be in this with you."

EXODUS 18:13–19 (MSG)

Your parents can help you see a better way through the heaviness and the hard stuff. I didn't go to my parents about important things, and it made me feel isolated and confused at times. But as an adult, I go to them often for advice and insight. I wish I had done it more growing up.

It's never healthy to keep things in, and your parents or guardian are the best people to share the hard stuff with. Let them in so they can help you.

1) Do you feel safe talking to your parents about your feelings? Why or why not?

2) If not, can you have a conversation with them to share your concerns and see if communication can be restored?

3) What is something you'd like to share with your parents that you have been keeping inside? How would you begin this conversation? Write down your train of thought and any good ideas you might have.

4) If you told them, how did it feel to stop carrying that burden?

PRAYER Jesus, I can't carry my feelings and the hard things in my life all by myself. I know You are there, and that makes me feel safe. But I also know You give us people to help us through life. Please give me the courage to talk about the hard things with my parents or guardian. I thank You for them and that I don't have to carry all the hard stuff alone. Amen.

Developing Trust

You will earn the trust and respect of others if you work for good; if you work for evil, you are making a mistake.

PROVERBS 14:22 (GNT)

You're at the age when you'll want more privacy. I remember that desire for sure! I asked for a telephone (with a cord, yes!) in my bedroom so that when friends called, I could talk to them privately. I tried to show my parents that I could be trusted with a phone by listening to them when they asked me to do something, staying on top of my chores without being asked, and babysitting my little brothers when they asked me to. I tried to find ways to show them I was responsible and that I could be trusted to do the right thing.

It is frustrating when you want a little more freedom, but it feels like your parents are pushing back. I'm going to let you in on a little secret: the more you listen to and respect your parents, the more they will trust you, and the more privacy and freedom they will feel you deserve.

Your parents need to trust you to give more space, and that's something you will have to earn. If you're always talking back to them and not doing your chores, your parents or guardian probably won't feel like they can trust you with more space. But if you listen to them and share with them things you're going through, you will earn their trust.

Even the Bible says that those who do good earn trust and respect, and those who do bad make mistakes. Show your parents that you are someone they can trust! And when you are given more freedom and privacy, be the person they, and God, hope you will be when they are not around.

1) **What does more freedom and privacy look like to you? For me, it was having a phone or being able to close my bedroom door.**
2) **What do you think your parents would say if you asked for this?**
3) **In what ways are your parents asking you to grow? In what areas do they want to see improvement?**
4) **How could you be more respectful toward your parents or guardian?**
5) **What are some things you can do to earn their trust?**

PRAYER God, I would like more space and trust as I grow up and get older. Help me to earn my parents' trust and show them I am someone they can give more freedom to. And when I earn those things, help me to honor them, and to honor You. Thank You for the freedoms You give us every day. It's in Your name I pray. Amen.

Friendships with Siblings

I grew up with three younger brothers; I was the only girl. Boy, did they pick on me, but to be fair, I picked on them too! As kids, we used to fight so much. We would scream and slam doors. I think we broke almost every door in our house. Yikes!

But you know what's really cool? My brothers are now my best friends. I tell them just about everything, and we often talk on the phone. They mean the world to me, even though they used to drive me crazy!

If you have any siblings, you know what I'm talking about. Sometimes a brother or sister can bug you more than anyone else. They know exactly which buttons to push.

All that fighting can make it hard for everyone at home. As grown-ups, some people don't feel a close connection with their siblings, especially if issues haven't been resolved or healing hasn't begun. Be mindful of how delicate relationships are and how constant fighting can wear down even the best relationships. Instead of focusing on what disconnects you from your siblings, find ways to connect. You could take an interest in one of their hobbies, find something fun to do together, or talk about some hard stuff you're going through.

Even when they make you really mad and you want to get back at them, choose to show them kindness instead. The brothers and sisters you have can be your best friends. One day, your relationship with them will be one of the best parts of your life!

1) Do you have a brother or sister, maybe even a few, who get on your nerves?

2) Describe a recent conflict that really upset you. What happened that made you feel hurt and defensive?

3) Did you ever work it out with them? How did it make you feel?

4) What kind of relationship do you want to have with them now and in the future?

5) How do you want to act next time you get mad at each other?

PRAYER Lord, I thank You for the siblings in my life. Even though we get mad at each other, I want them to be my friends, and I want to treat them kindly. Please help us keep the peace. Even when they aren't kind to me, help me be kind to them. Amen.

Finding Your Friends

Two people are better off than one, for they can help each other succeed. If one person falls, the other can reach out and help. But someone who falls alone is in real trouble.

ECCLESIASTES 4:9–10 (NLT)

Friendships make life rich and meaningful. God wants us to all be living in community, and He tells us this often in the Bible. The Trinity—Father, Son, and Holy Spirit—all exist within a community. When God created man, He saw it was not good for man to be alone and He created a woman to be a companion to him. In the book of Ecclesiastes, which was written by the wisest man who ever lived, God says we should have good relationships.

Having good friends gives you someone to talk to when life takes you on its twists and turns. It gives you people who will have your back in times of need, and others to laugh with and celebrate the joys.

Solomon, the man who wrote Ecclesiastes, talks about how a friend can help you succeed but can also be there to catch you when you fall. That's the kind of person you want to have in your life.

But it's about more than just having friends. Just anyone will not do. You need friends who love God and are kind to others. People who pressure you to do things you know aren't right or ignore you when times are tough are not the kind of friends who have your best interest at heart.

There is a saying that goes, "Show me your friends and I'll show you your future." The people you choose to be with can influence the kind of person you become. Find good, godly, kind friends who will help you become the best version of yourself.

1) What does a good friend look like to you? List the qualities that you admire and value.

2) Do you know people with these qualities and values who you want to be closer to? How will you reach out to them and establish a connection?

3) Think about the friends in your life right now. Are there any who don't share the same love for Jesus or just don't have the same qualities and priorities as you do? What makes you friends with them, and should you consider moving on to healthier relationships? Explain.

4) For those friends who haven't given themselves to Jesus yet, how can you be a light and witness to them? How can you help point them to God's path?

PRAYER Jesus, thank You for being my friend. You are definitely the best friend I could ever have! I know friendships are important to You and that You want me to have good friends. Will You help me build a community of friends who love You and are good to others? Please give me wisdom in choosing my companions. Amen.

Real Friends

My ten-year-old niece Abigail and I had a really good conversation about what makes a good friend. She is navigating some of her friendships and has started to realize that some of the girls she knows aren't the real friends she thought they were.

These so-called friends were talking behind her back and ignoring her texts. When she asked these girls to hang out, they never had time. Abigail is starting to see them in a different light—people whom she thought were her friends but are actually unkind.

This has been hard for her, but it is also helping her to see who her true friends are. By losing some people in her life, Abigail has started to find her core group of good friends.

We all have friends who come and go. Sometimes, we just lose touch with people as we get older. Others we have to let go because they have hurt us too much. My best friend hurt me really bad last year, and I'm an adult! It happens, unfortunately. And while losing friends can hurt, it can also help you find your true friends.

The reality is that the friends you lose are probably not the ones you can rely on, no matter how much fun they are to be around. Proverbs tells us that if we surround ourselves with good people, we are more influenced to be good and do good.

How a person treats you and others can say a lot about them. Examine your friendships by listening to the way people talk about others to you and how they talk about you to others. See how responsive they are to you. Do they answer your texts or calls in a timely manner or eventually get back to you if they are preoccupied? Do they want to spend quality time with you? Last but not least, do they love and respect God? If they haven't given themselves fully to God and you have, how can you be a witness to them without them influencing your life?

As for Abigail, she is now able to focus on getting to know her true friends better and has a stronger support system because of these solid friendships.

1) Have you lost or let go of some people in your life who you thought were friends? What happened that made you realize they were not the people you thought they were?

2) How did you respond to losing their friendship?

3) Who are the real friends in your life? How can you better invest in your true friends?

4) Are you a quality friend to the people in your life? How can you do better and show how much you truly care about these friendships?

PRAYER God, thank You for the authentic friends in my life. And even though people have hurt me, I trust that it's better they are not in my life anymore. Help me to attract and focus on real friends. Give me eyes to see and ears to hear who You want me to be good friends with. Amen.

WEEK 29 What's the Deal with Cliques?

Cliques can be good and bad. Good because people have found other people they enjoy being with. But they also can be bad when those in the clique are mean to others outside the group.

If I could encourage you to do one thing for others, I would say be kind. Kindness is one of the most beautiful gifts anyone could ever receive.

In today's passage in Romans, we see examples of how to treat people and how not to treat people.

⭐ ***Do good and not harm to those unlike you.*** We are all different, but that doesn't mean we can't get along. Be good to all, even those who aren't like you.

⭐ ***Share in the ups and downs with your friends.*** Being a great friend means being there for your friends. When something good happens to them, be excited for them and celebrate with them. When they are going through something sad, offer empathy and support.

> *Bless your enemies; no cursing under your breath. Laugh with your happy friends when they're happy; share tears when they're down. Get along with each other; don't be stuck-up. Make friends with nobodies; don't be the great somebody. Don't hit back; discover beauty in everyone. If you've got it in you, get along with everybody.*
>
> **ROMANS 12:14–18 (MSG)**

* *Be nice to everyone.* And that means everyone, especially the people everyone else picks on.
* *Everyone is valuable; nobody is better than anyone else.* Not even the popular people. No one person is better than another. Everyone has value.
* *See the good in everyone.* This applies even to those who act mean. Chances are, they are acting out because they are hurting inside. Showing them kindness might help them bring down those walls.

Honor God and set the example by showing your peers what a good person looks like.

1) What are your thoughts on cliques? Good or bad, or both?
2) Have you been hurt by a clique? What happened and how did it make you feel?
3) Do you have a close group of friends? Who is in this group?
4) Do you think your group is good to others or can they sometimes be unkind to those on the outside?
5) How do you want to treat people who are not in your group of friends?

PRAYER Father, thank You for the friends You have put into my life. I'm so glad to have people I can do life with. Will You please help me to be okay when people hurt me, and help me not hurt others? Help me to be a person who is kind, warm, and inviting to all. I want to be like You, loving people well. Amen.

The Harm Bullies Cause

Watch the way you talk. Let nothing foul or dirty come out of your mouth. Say only what helps, each word a gift.

EPHESIANS 4:29 (MSG)

Bullying is one of the worst things. I remember being bullied in middle school, especially by this one kid named Tyler. He was in my grade and always sat at the back of the bus. But he would call me names and make fun of me a lot, and it hurt. It made me doubt my value and self-worth.

I never stood up to him, and I let him treat me that way. And he continued to do so for many years. Today, I wish I had said something to him back then.

Maybe you've been bullied. It hurts, doesn't it? It makes you feel bad about yourself and question your value.

Bullying is usually an indication of the person doing the bullying. Hurt people hurt people. Bullies are mean to others because they themselves are hurting inside. It doesn't make it right by any means, but I hope this explanation helps you to understand that it's really not about you. It's the bully's own hurt that causes them to lash out.

In a later devotion, we're going to talk about what to do when someone hurts you. But if you are being bullied, don't stay silent. Please tell your parents and a teacher so they can help you. Bullying, when gone unchecked, can have negative, long-term effects on your mental health and self-esteem. Bullying should be nipped in the bud.

I would encourage you to talk to the bully. I know that can seem scary, and it might not always make the bullying stop, but you are worth standing up for. Completely worth it. I wish I had allowed myself the voice to tell my bully how his actions and words made me feel, and I wish I would have asked him to stop. I can't change that now, but you can stand up.

Now I want to flip it on you. Please don't ever bully someone or cause someone to feel bad about themselves. Words hurt. And maybe you don't say a mean thing to someone's face, but saying it behind their back is still hurtful.

Ephesians 4:29 warns us not to use bad or hurtful words, but only words that build others up. Use your words to do good, not harm. Be a gift, not a weapon. Be known as the person who speaks highly of others and lifts them up!

1) Have you ever been bullied? What happened, and how did it make you feel?

2) Are you being bullied right now? Who can you talk to about it?

3) Do you feel like you could talk to the kid bullying you about it? What would you say?

4) Have you ever bullied someone? What hurt are you feeling that is making you lash out like this?

PRAYER Jesus, bullying is so hurtful, and I know when You see it, it hurts Your heart. Please help me to heal from the wounds others have inflicted upon me and give me the courage to talk about it. And I ask that You please help me to be a kind person who does not use my words to hurt others. Help me to guard my mouth, Lord. Amen.

WEEK 31 Resisting Peer Pressure

Peer pressure is at its peak at your age. You may be feeling pushed and pulled to act a certain way, dress a certain way, or try new things that you don't feel very good about. All this can weigh heavily on you.

What do you do when your peers try to get you to do things that don't feel right?

First, remember Who you serve and Who you aim to please. The Bible tells us we can only serve one master—either God or the world. Serving the world means giving in to peer pressure and going against what God wants for you. If you choose to serve God, pleasing Him should be the most important thing in the world to you.

Second, be in the Bible, for it gives you strength to resist. In fact, the Word of God is your weapon to fight temptation. Even Jesus quoted Scripture to defeat Satan when Satan tempted Jesus into sin. The Bible tells us that we can use God's Word to fight off temptation. Spending time reading the Bible will help you fight peer pressure.

Remember: the more you know the Bible and know God, the more you will love Him. And when you love Him, you want to obey Him rather than the world.

Third, surround yourself with friends who love God. Godly friends can encourage you to do the right thing when others try to get you to do the wrong thing. It's also why going to church is so important. The Church—people who follow God—can encourage each other!

When you feel pressured by others to do something that feels wrong, pray to God and ask Him to help you in those moments.

1) Have you ever been pressured by your peers and done what they told you to do? How did it make you feel afterward?

2) How can one work to serve God more than the world? Can you give a personal example where you had to choose and it was difficult for you?

3) What is one Bible verse you can memorize that will help you be strong in moments of peer pressure?

4) Who can be the first person you talk to when pressured to do something wrong?

5) Of the three things described above that can help you fight peer pressure, which one do you think you need to work on the most?

PRAYER God, I really want to honor You with my life and do the right thing. Will You please help me to be strong in those moments when I am tempted by my peers to do something I know is wrong? Please give me the strength to do what You would want me to do. I love You so much and want to follow You with my whole heart, honoring You with my life. Amen.

WEEK 32 # The Trap of Compromise

There are so many things I've done that I wish I could take back. People I've hurt with words, actions that cost me big-time, and dreams lost. There's so much I wish I could say to twelve-year-old Brittany about what's to come and how to live well, but I can't.

You're going to make mistakes because we're all human and far from perfect. The Father knew we were not perfect before He even created us, so He also made a plan for reconciliation between humanity and Himself. He sent His only Son, Jesus, to die for our sins. Jesus' sinless body carried every single sin you and I would ever commit for redemption through His blood.

But just because Jesus made a way to redeem us doesn't mean we should live our lives recklessly. This gift of salvation from sin is only for those who love Him more than anyone or anything and who truly want to follow Him in obedience.

Hurtful words can cost you a best friend. Giving in to peer pressure can cost you peace and safety. My two biggest regrets cost me dream jobs, and even though I know God uses everything for good, I still carry regret for my poor decisions.

Don't throw away a relationship, dream, peace, your reputation, or any good thing for momentary satisfaction. Sin is never worth its cost—I promise you that.

Stay close to Jesus, seek His wisdom, and make positive choices. You won't regret living fully for God!

1) Have you ever done something you know you shouldn't do and then felt bad afterward? What was it?

2) Were you able to work through the consequences, or do you still feel bad about it?

3) Do you believe that God can work everything together, the good and the bad, for good?

4) How have you seen Him work something bad out for good?

5) Is there someone you can talk to when things get hard or when you're feeling pressured to do the wrong thing? This is called "accountability" and can be really helpful. Who is this friend?

PRAYER Jesus, I know I will make mistakes, even though I don't want to. But I also know You are there for me and I thank You so much for Your love and grace. Thank You for taking my every sin on Yourself and redeeming my life. Please help me to lean into You and trust You, living for You alone. I love You so much. Amen.

Boys Are Confusing

> Promise me, O women of Jerusalem, not to awaken love until the time is right.
>
> **SONG OF SOLOMON 8:4 (NLT)**

Do you ever wonder how to act around boys? Especially the one you have a crush on? And what to do with these feelings you have? Let me just ease any anxiety you may have and say that this is all very normal. Even back in my preteen days, when I would have sleepovers with my friends, we all got a little nervous around boys.

Want to know something that sounds really simple but can actually be really hard? Just be yourself! You should never change who you are for someone. If you stay true to yourself, you'll find that it's much easier to navigate your feelings. Because when you know who you are and that you won't change for a person, you'll find the right people to be around. People, boys included, will want to be around you for who you are rather than someone you're not.

Another important rule to live by is not rushing feelings or relationships, especially at an age where everyone, even boys, are trying to figure out the kind of person they want to be.

You have years to learn about feelings and how to handle them well. The Bible tells us to not awaken love before it's time. Meaning, don't rush into dating or love. Figure out who you are, learn to navigate emotions, and surround yourself with godly people. From this healthy place, down the road, something will work out with a good person.

In the meantime, learn how to work through feelings and build friendships. Talk to your parents or a trusted adult about your feelings for boys. How do they feel about the potential of a boy wanting to be your boyfriend? Trusting this journey with your parents or guardian might seem weird, but it can actually be so good for you.

1) Is there a boy you have a crush on right now? What qualities do you like best about this person?

2) What qualities do you value most in people?

3) Do you talk about this (or any) crush and feelings with someone? Who, and why that person?

4) What kind of relationship would you want for yourself, and how would you like to be treated? Establish strong standards and convictions for yourself, and list them.

5) How might boys be a distraction in your life? Is that distraction worth it?

PRAYER God, having feelings for boys at this age is normal, and I know I'm not alone. It seems like my friends talk about it, and it's something I should want—a boyfriend. And maybe I do. But I also don't want to rush into anything that isn't good for me. I ask that You please help me work through my feelings to get to a good place. Help me not to get so focused on boys that I miss all the good things You want for me right now. I trust You, God. Amen.

When People Hurt You

The Lord is near to the brokenhearted and saves the crushed in spirit.

PSALM 34:18 (ESV)

Pain is a part of our lives, and that's because sin is in the world. And in those moments when people hurt you, it can feel pretty lonely.

When I was in high school, I took a trip with the dance team to a competition. I had taken my journal with me to write in while on the long bus ride. I ended up falling asleep, and one of the older girls grabbed my journal and started reading it. Then she told some of the other girls what I wrote in it. Some of it was really personal, and I even mentioned how some of my teammates had hurt me.

Everyone on the team either got mad at me or made fun of me for what I had shared in my personal journal, and it hurt me so much. They were some of my closest friends, and now they'd invaded my very personal feelings, leaving me vulnerable and embarrassed. I was so sad, and it led to an unpleasant few months for me.

We have this promise—yes, a promise you can count on—that God is near to those who have a broken heart and crushed spirit. So, when you feel alone, God reminds you that you aren't.

If you're hurting now, I am so sorry you're in pain. Please know God is holding you close to Him and that this pain won't last forever.

For the trouble and hurts to come, place them in God's hands. He wants you to run to Him for safety. To talk to Him about your hurt feelings and have faith He will make things better.

God has you, and He will not leave you or abandon you.

1) Have you ever been hurt by someone? How did that make you feel?
2) Are you hurting now? What happened?
3) What gives you comfort from reading this devotion?
4) Do you feel safe to share your feelings with God and believe He will care for you?
5) Can you talk to someone about your worries in life?

PRAYER Father, thank You for this promise that You will be near to me when I'm hurting. You are so good and faithful to me, and I know I don't deserve it. I love You so much and give my heart to You. Every pain and feeling I trust You with. Please heal my heart when it hurts and bring good to the bad. Amen.

Forgiveness

I'm so sorry for the pain you are going to face in this world. But as hard as these experiences can be, they also hold so much value in your spiritual growth. If you'll lean into them, you will be refined into a beautiful woman of God.

Make allowance for each other's faults, and forgive anyone who offends you. Remember, the Lord forgave you, so you must forgive others.

COLOSSIANS 3:13 (NLT)

What do we do when people hurt us? Is it okay to stay mad and bitter? The Bible tells us no, and my own personal experience says the same. When we hold that kind of hurt in, it ends up damaging you more than the other person. Anger and hate are poison that slowly chips away at your heart.

When someone hurts you, choosing to forgive may be the most challenging thing to do, especially if they don't apologize or ask for forgiveness, but choosing to forgive is the best thing you can do for yourself. In fact, Jesus commands us to forgive multiple times in the New Testament. In today's passage, He tells us to forgive anyone who offends us because we have been forgiven.

You see, we don't deserve forgiveness, yet Jesus forgives us. If He can forgive you and me for all our sins, can't we forgive someone who has hurt us? Who are we to withhold forgiveness, when we've received the greatest gift of all?

I know it's hard when people say something cruel or do something spiteful behind your back. But you can find healing from such pain. It starts in the arms of Jesus and continues through forgiveness.

And let me share this, because I didn't know it for a long time: you might have to forgive someone for the same thing more than once. I encourage you, every time that hurt pops up and you find bitterness seeping in, forgive again. Forgive as many times as you need to.

1) Has someone hurt you? What happened?
2) How did that hurt make you feel?
3) Are you having a hard time forgiving them, or have you already done so?
4) If you haven't forgiven them yet, why?
5) How will you pursue forgiveness?

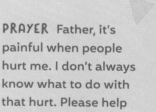

PRAYER Father, it's painful when people hurt me. I don't always know what to do with that hurt. Please help me to have a heart that forgives, as You have asked me to do. Especially when it's hard to do so. Thank You for forgiving me when I've never deserved it and I could never earn it. I love You, God. Amen.

PART FOUR

Feelings & Identity

Feeling Good in Your Skin

For we are God's masterpiece. He has created us anew in Christ Jesus, so we can do the good things he planned for us long ago.

EPHESIANS 2:10 (NLT)

I felt so awkward at your age. Back then, we didn't have social media or YouTube makeup and hair tutorials. I had no older sisters to show me how to do either, and my mom wasn't very helpful in that department. I was pale with frizzy hair and had no idea how to work with what I had. In fact, I used to get picked on for my fair skin and dark hair, because it reminded kids of a popular male rock star back in the day.

All to say, I get it. It can feel really weird to be in a preteen body and wrestle with body image. You are not alone, beautiful girl!

Your body is changing and maturing, and that can make you feel uncomfortable or dissatisfied. You might find yourself comparing your body to that of other girls around you, or on television and online, perhaps feeling disappointed about how you look.

God wants you to know that He thinks you are beautiful, and He created you as a great masterpiece. You were designed by Him in your mother's womb, and every detail was planned. You are stunning!

Please don't ever doubt your value or your worth. Be healthy, yes, but give more attention to your character than your body. Choose to spend hours reading the Bible and being in prayer rather than watching videos or shows that only leave you discouraged.

Remember what Proverbs 31:30 says: "Charm is deceptive, and beauty does not last; but a woman who fears the Lord will be greatly praised" (NLT).

1) Do you have any concerns about how you look? Write these down and pray about them.
2) Do you find yourself comparing yourself to other girls? Does that usually make you feel better or worse about yourself?
3) Do you have someone you can talk to about these insecurities?
4) What are some ways you can reset and get to a better place when you start comparing yourself?
5) What do you like most about your personality?

PRAYER Father, thank You for taking the time and care to make me; I know You put great detail and attention into my making. I struggle sometimes to feel confident in my skin, or I find myself comparing my body to other girls' and it makes me feel bad. But I don't want to do that, and I need Your help. Please help me to find my identity in You, focus on my inward heart, and appreciate the health that You have given me. Amen.

Be Younique

Abby was in fifth grade and in a place where she was trying to figure out who she is and where she fits in the world. She tried to fit in by being like everyone else. She would wear name-brand clothes, like the characters in the cool movies everyone else liked, and wear makeup. But it ended up leaving Abby discouraged.

Abby decided to talk to her mom about what she was going through, and her mom gave her something really important to think about. She said, "You can't be someone else, but you can be you. So, be yourself!"

Abby had been wanting a pair of blue glasses, but at first, she felt like she needed another look to fit in. She kept looking at other girls' styles in glasses in order to figure out what was most popular. But after talking to her mom, she decided to get the glasses she *really* wanted. And ever since, Abby has been rocking those glasses!

Girls your age often want to fit in. There is nothing wrong with the desire to be part of a community, but you shouldn't forfeit your identity in the process. Take it from my own experiences: trying to emulate everyone else—being someone you're not—is exhausting

Don't become so well-adjusted to your culture that you fit into it without even thinking. Instead, fix your attention on God. You'll be changed from the inside out. Readily recognize what he wants from you, and quickly respond to it. Unlike the culture around you, always dragging you down to its level of immaturity, God brings the best out of you, develops well-formed maturity in you.

ROMANS 12:1–2 (MSG)

and discouraging. God didn't create us all to look and act the same, but rather, He created us to be unique! If you're trying to be like someone else, you'll miss the special and important way God wants to use you.

Be the daughter of the King that He created you to be, using the gifts and passions He has given you. If you want to try to be like someone, then try to be like Him!

1) Do you catch yourself acting differently from who you really are or wearing something you don't really love just because you want to be liked and accepted? If so, how does this realization make you feel? What does it make you want to do?

2) What would you do or wear differently if you allowed yourself to be just you?

3) Is there something you want to try, but you're afraid of what others will think?

4) What gifts and passions has God given you?

PRAYER Dear Lord, thank You for making me and putting so much thought into my design. Sometimes I find myself getting lost trying to be like everyone else. But I want to be comfortable in my own skin and in who You created me to be. Please help me to remain faithful to You and Your design, and to live in the personality, gifts, and passions You have given me. Amen.

Change Is Hard

"For I know the plans I have for you," says the Lord. "They are plans for good and not for disaster, to give you a future and a hope."

JEREMIAH 29:11 (NLT)

We've talked about how hard this season can be, with puberty and all the changes taking place in your life. And change can be scary.

I remember being so scared of transitioning from elementary school to junior high, and then again from junior high to high school. It meant meeting new people and finding my place in all of it.

Change is a part of life, and it will happen. But it doesn't have to be terrifying with God on your side. He can see everything that will ever happen. He knows everything about your life, even what will happen in ten, or even fifty years. He can see the future! He knows what is best for you, and He makes plans for your life that are good and helpful.

You don't have to be afraid because God knows everything and wants to use every part of your life for good. Even the hard and messy things in life, when turned over to God, can be used for good.

When I didn't make the cheer squad in junior high, God had another plan that was better. And He can do that in your life. The changes that come aren't a surprise to Him, and if you'll trust Him, God will lead you into great purpose.

1) What kind of changes are you most nervous about for the future? Describe these fears and why you think you have them.

2) Do you believe that God can guide you and use you for His good? How do you know He is there for you?

3) What are some areas in your life that you need to trust God with more?

4) Who can you talk to when you feel apprehensive about change?

5) Have you ever seen God use something hard or bad for good in the long run? What was it?

PRAYER God, there are so many changes in life, and sometimes it scares me. I don't always like change, and I'm not always sure how to face it. Will You please help me to trust You with my life and trust Your plans? I know You are good, and You want good for me. Amen.

WEEK 39 Overwhelming Emotions

Don't worry about anything; instead, pray about everything. Tell God what you need and thank him for all he has done. Then you will experience God's peace, which exceeds anything we can understand. His peace will guard your hearts and minds as you live in Christ Jesus.

PHILIPPIANS 4:6–7 (NLT)

People are capable of expressing a whole rainbow of feelings—happiness, sadness, anger, loneliness, anxiety, and excitement, to name only a few. It can be hard to work through all the different emotions we go through. How do you calm down when you're really angry? Or how do you find joy when you're sad? Even as an adult, I still struggle with managing my emotions.

There's hope, though! God created every single emotion and feels them too, which means if there is anyone who gets it and can help, it's Him.

I really like today's verse because it reminds me what I should do when I'm feeling something and don't know how to work through it. God tells us to pray about it. Tell Him what you feel and what you need, and He will help you. God can give you peace, no matter what you're feeling.

Oh, and one more thing: give thanks! I know it's sometimes hard to praise God when you're sad or anxious, but that's exactly when we should praise. Because praise unlocks something inside of us that helps us to trust God.

I also want to encourage you to talk to an older godly person, like a parent or guardian, about emotions you have that feel over-whelming. It's not healthy to keep your feelings inside. Someone you trust can help you navigate through any struggles you are having.

Don't be afraid of your feelings, however overwhelming they may be. Instead, pray to God to help you process them in a healthy way.

1) What's a feeling you have a hard time expressing or working through when it pops up? Why do you think this is?

2) Is there a feeling you have now, or is there something you are worried about, that you want to work through?

3) Write a prayer to God about how you're feeling and why you need Him.

4) Is there a trusted adult you can talk to when you need help with challenging emotions or personal decisions? Who is this person, and what makes them trustworthy?

5) How will you remember to thank God even when it's hard?

PRAYER Jesus, I have a lot of feelings, and sometimes I don't know what to do with them. I know I shouldn't keep them all in. Will You please help me work through these emotions and give me peace when I come to You with them? And help me to remember to praise You when I'm feeling overwhelmed. Thank You for helping me, Lord. Amen.

Share Your Sadness

Give all your worries and cares to God, for he cares about you.

1 PETER 5:7 (NLT)

Sadness is a part of this life, unfortunately. We can't escape it, but praise the Lord, we do have Someone we can escape to when we are sad.

When I was your age, I was often sad. I felt a lot of anger and loneliness growing up in my home. And I didn't know God. I was all by myself with all that sadness, and bottling it up made life harder for me. I was angry and depressed because of it.

But when I met Jesus as a teenager, for the first time in my life, I didn't feel alone anymore. I had Someone to share my sadness with. It was freeing and healing!

You have Him too, my friend. When someone says something mean to you, you can tell God about it. When you get into a fight with your family, He can help you work through that. If you don't make the team at school or get the grade you want, God is there for you. He is there for you when a friend abandons you, or if someone you love dies, or if your parents decide to live separately. Your problems can be as big as any adult's problems, but know that God is listening.

Our sadness doesn't have to be bottled up inside, but rather, we can bring all of it to Jesus. And the cool thing is, He wants us to! Our sadness is never too much for God. That's what we see in today's Bible verse—that God cares so much for you that He wants you to bring your worries and concerns to Him. You don't have to carry them alone. He can help you work through them, so you don't have to be sad anymore. There is no better place to find joy and peace than in Jesus!

It was only when I finally gave my sadness to Jesus that it started to fade away. He can do the same for you too.

1) Are you carrying sadness right now? What do you think the source of that sadness is?

2) What have you done so far to try to resolve the sadness?

3) Have you talked to God about it? If not, what would you like to say to Him?

4) What actions do you need to take to manage this feeling?

5) Find a Bible verse that gives you peace when you're sad and write it down.

PRAYER Jesus, I get sad sometimes, but I also know You have felt sadness and can help me with it. I don't want to be alone in feeing sad. I want to share my problems with You, so we can fix them together. Please help me to remember to always share my feelings with You, and please help me when I feel this way. Thank You, Jesus. Amen.

Feeling Alone

Growing up, I often felt alone. I wasn't very close to my parents, I fought with my younger brothers a lot, and I didn't have many friends or close family. And then Jesus came into my life, and all that changed! Not only did I have Him—the best gift of all—but my circle of friends began to grow, and my relationships grew stronger. God totally changed my life!

Even now, I sometimes still struggle with loneliness, but God helps me with that. One of my favorite passages to turn to when I feel alone is this one, in Isaiah 43.

You have this beautiful promise from God that, when you feel like you're drowning, He will rescue you. When you feel overwhelmed, He is there for you. And when you feel scared and alone in the fire, He will make sure you won't be burned.

What this means is, no matter how deep the valley you must travel, for the person who loves God, they always have access to Him. God is with His children, no matter where they are or what they're going through.

You are not alone. Even though you can't see Him, God is with you in your troubles. He goes before you, walks with you, and has your back every step in the storm.

Will you go to Him and find refuge for your loneliness in His care? He loves you so much and wants to take care of you, but He does ask that you trust Him. Will you?

1) Have you ever felt alone? Why did you feel that way?
2) What did you do when you felt alone? Did you go to someone, or withdraw into yourself?
3) What about this verse gives you hope and encouragement?
4) Do you trust God, that He is with you even when you don't feel it? Explain why or why not.
5) The next time you feel alone, what will you do to cope?

PRAYER Oh Father, being lonely is so hard, and I feel hopeless sometimes. But I know I'm not truly alone because You are with me. Even in the darkest valleys, You comfort me. Thank You for loving me and taking care of me, Jesus. I put my trust in You! Amen.

The Power of Fear

Don't panic. I'm with you. There's no need to fear for I'm your God. I'll give you strength. I'll help you. I'll hold you steady, keep a firm grip on you.

ISAIAH 41:10 (MSG)

Were you ever afraid of the dark or of monsters under your bed when you were little? I was, and now, I have a three-year-old boy who is. We can be so afraid of what we can't see, working ourselves up over it. I can tell my son daily that monsters aren't real and that Jesus will keep him safe, and even though he's never seen a monster, he is convinced there is one in his closet.

I wish I could sit with you over some hot chocolate or lemonade and talk with you about your fears. Are you afraid of not being accepted at school? Perhaps you're afraid you won't be taken care of at home or that your parents won't always be there. Whatever it is you fear, I'd look you in the eyes right now, if I could, and tell you that fear is real, but often what we fear isn't. And that you serve the God Who no one and nothing can overcome!

God talks about fear throughout the Bible because He knows we feel it and that it's a very real emotion for us. He wants us to know that, one, we don't have to be afraid, and, two, He is with us and will take care of us.

When I'm afraid, I take my eyes off the fear and put them on God, praying the name of Jesus specifically because I know there is power in His name. And that's what I hope you'll do too.

Our fears have power only when we focus on them. Take your eyes off the fearful situation and put them on God, and you'll see the fear subside. It's truly a powerful and remarkable feat to watch your fears vanish in the presence of God!

1) What are some of your greatest fears? Why do you think you have them?

2) Do you see them as something to truly fear, or do you think you could be giving them too much power over you? Explain.

3) How does your fear size up next to God?

4) Next time you're afraid, what will you do to cope?

PRAYER Oh Lord, I've been afraid, and I'm not a fan of it. I'm so grateful that nothing is too powerful to overcome You, and that when I am afraid, I can turn to You for comfort and strength. Please help me to turn my eyes to You when fear comes calling and help me to trust You with everything. It's in Your name I pray. Amen.

WEEK 43 Worry and Anxiety

My biggest worry when I was a preteen was being accepted by the other kids at school. I desperately wanted to be popular, and because I wasn't, it made me anxious, especially when the boy-who-shall-not-be-named picked on me when riding the bus.

We live in an anxiety-filled world. Look at this passage in Matthew 6. Just before these verses, Jesus is talking about how unbelievers often worry about what they will eat and wear. Seeking after the things of this world was, and is, something nonbelievers do.

But you and I believe in God and should have different priorities. We aren't to worry about the things of this world—like being accepted by everyone at school or having the coolest clothes—rather, we should seek the Kingdom of God. What this looks like is choosing to obey God, living right, and pleasing Him.

Ask yourself: Are you craving to walk in obedience and holiness (which means to be

So don't worry about these things, saying, "What will we eat? What will we drink? What will we wear?" These things dominate the thoughts of unbelievers, but your heavenly Father already knows all your needs. Seek the Kingdom of God above all else, and live righteously, and he will give you everything you need. So don't worry about tomorrow, for tomorrow will bring its own worries. Today's trouble is enough for today.

MATTHEW 6:31–34 (NLT)

set apart) over the things of this world? Wouldn't you rather be set apart because you love God rather than be like everyone else?

If you do, God will meet not only your physical needs, but your eternal ones as well. He will go above and beyond in caring for you! You don't have to worry because God takes care of the details.

So, next time you find yourself worrying, seek God and walk in obedience through worship and surrender. You'll find your worry and anxiety subside as you do!

1) What causes you to worry and feel anxious?
2) In what ways do you cope with those feelings?
3) What do you think you can and will do differently to fight these emotions?
4) How can you keep God first in your life?
5) In what ways can you be walking in obedience that you aren't now?

PRAYER Jesus, I love You so much and thank You for taking care of me. I don't have to worry because You provide for all my needs, both here and in eternity. Will You please help me to not get anxious about the things in my life and to turn to You when I do? Thank You, God! Amen.

PART FIVE

The World vs. God

WEEK 44 Eyes Off the World

Many things that go on in this world can seem overwhelming and a bit terrifying—violence, disease, and natural disasters, just to name a few. And sometimes they can make you and me feel afraid and worried. What do we do when we see all these terrible things happening?

It really helps me to get my eyes off the situation, put them on Jesus, and remind myself that this is not my home. You see, our home is in heaven with God. This world and our time here is temporary. In heaven, there is no pain or suffering or sadness. Eternity will be spent there, in absolute perfect harmony with God and His family.

Until then, we remind ourselves and accept that we are born into a sinful world—we can't escape it on earth. So, instead of stressing out about catastrophic events and situations you cannot control, turn to Jesus, and focus on doing good, like He did in His time on earth. Love those around you, adopt praise, and give thanks to Him for taking care of you in the middle of the hard stuff.

> For there is no city here on earth that will last forever. We are looking for the one that is coming. Let us give thanks all the time to God through Jesus Christ. Our gift to Him is to give thanks. Our lips should always give thanks to His name.
>
> **HEBREWS 13:14–15 (NLV)**

1) Is there something going on in this world right now that worries you? What is it?
2) Have you talked to someone about it? How are you handling the worry?
3) How does this verse encourage you?
4) Next time something scary happens, what will you do?
5) What can you be thankful for today?

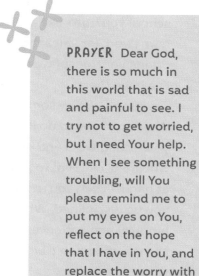

PRAYER Dear God, there is so much in this world that is sad and painful to see. I try not to get worried, but I need Your help. When I see something troubling, will You please remind me to put my eyes on You, reflect on the hope that I have in You, and replace the worry with praise? Thank You, Lord. Amen.

School, Homework, and Academics

School isn't always fun or easy. I was the typical student with Bs and Cs (and the occasional A) because I never really applied myself. Math was terrible, and don't even get me started on science!

If you're anything like I was, there's probably something about school you don't like all that much. Perhaps the never-ending homework (or at least it seems that way, right?), sitting in class during your least favorite subjects, the struggle to keep up . . . Yep, I've been there!

But you know something I wish I had known at your age? You don't have to do it alone. It's true! God can help you with your schoolwork and with the stress of it all. When you feel over-whelmed, ask Him to give you peace so you can focus on the tasks at hand. When you're falling behind in a class, pray for Him to help you be disciplined. When a subject doesn't make sense, ask for humility and patience. Then, reach out to your teacher or parent. He can use the people around you to help you succeed. You don't have to do this alone!

God can give you insight and discipline that is rooted in godly wisdom to help you navigate school and academics. It's right there for you—you simply need to ask for it.

So, will you go to the Father and ask Him for His wisdom to help you through your school years? It could make all the difference for you!

1) What kind of academic struggles do you have with school?
2) Do they feel manageable, or do they make you feel stressed?
3) What can you do to help relieve some of that pressure? Have you already talked to a parent or teacher or considered getting a tutor?
4) How could you use God's help in school?
5) How would you describe wisdom? How can you pray for wisdom?

PRAYER Father, thank You for the wisdom You have and are willing to impart to us. School feels hard sometimes, and I need Your help with it. I would like Your wisdom to help me through my classes, homework, and schedule and managing it all. I put my trust in You for school and ask that You would please help me, God. Thank You in advance for helping me, Lord. Amen.

WEEK 46 Balancing Extra Activities

I grew up dancing, first in my beginner classes at six, and then into my teen years as a member of the dance team at school. More often than not, it was an escape for me and an outlet for my stress. But with it, came bad influences and a false sense of identity wrapped into the activity.

Extracurricular activities can be fun; it's why we do them! But sometimes, if we're not careful, they can become distractions or something we idolize too much, turning into sources of unhealthy obsession, stress, and worry.

Do you have a hobby? Does it get in the way of your peace or your relationship with God? Here are a few more key questions to ask yourself:

1) An idol—are you giving more time to this activity over God or desiring it more than you desire God?
2) A distraction—does it get in the way of church and/or school or eat up all your time, leaving you exhausted?
3) A worry—is this activity starting to stress you out and not feel fun anymore?

If you said yes to any of these three questions, then it could very well be time to give up the activity, or rethink the amount of time or energy you devote to it, if that is a possibility. If you're able to maintain a healthy balance, then keep enjoying this activity and passion. Just remember to do it all for the glory of God (1 Corinthians 10:31). In fact, everything you do should be for His glory!

And if you're wondering how to prioritize the things in your life, here's what I suggest:

GOD > FAMILY AND FRIENDS > CHURCH > SCHOOL > HOBBIES

1) What fun extracurricular activity do you participate in?
2) Has it become an idol in your life? If so, in what way? If not, how are you keeping it from being one?
3) Is it a distraction from your priorities? Why or why not?
4) Does it ever make you feel stressed, or does it feel hard to enjoy it sometimes?
5) Are there any changes you need to make in this area of your life (i.e., give up the activity or find an activity you would enjoy more)?

PRAYER Father, thank You for creating ways to enjoy life and for giving me the opportunity to express myself and use my gifts. As much as I like [insert your activity here], I never want it to become an idol, a distraction, or a worry. If it does, please give me the clarity and courage to let go of it. I want to honor You with it, do it for Your glory, and give it to You to use (or not use) how You'd like. In Jesus' name I pray. Amen.

WEEK 47 Living in a Tech World

Technology is all around us. It's in our hands, our homes, and everywhere we look. We can't get away from it, that's for sure! While it has so many good uses and benefits, being constantly connected and being addicted to your devices can get in the way of living a real life. With your eyes always on your screen, you can miss the beauty right in front of you—people, nature, places, experiences, and feelings filling your life with depth, joy, and adventure.

Technology can also be a source of trauma and stress. There is a lot of toxic content online, things people, and especially kids, shouldn't be exposed to. For preteens and teens, social media can be an unsafe space.

What do you think about tech? Do you ever find it to be draining or unhelpful? Perhaps you should look at how you can limit tech's reach in your life.

If you're struggling academically because you're constantly distracted by TV and media and addicted to your phone, make it a habit to study and do your homework as soon as you get home from school. Keep the TV off and put away all devices until you're

So if you're serious about living this new resurrection life with Christ, act like it. Pursue the things over which Christ presides. Don't shuffle along, eyes to the ground, absorbed with the things right in front of you. Look up, and be alert to what is going on around Christ—that's where the action is. See things from his perspective.

COLOSSIANS 3:1–2 (MSG)

done. Maybe you're also having a hard time sleeping because you're scrolling on your phone before bed, which then affects your ability to stay awake, focused, and engaged. Try putting the phone down thirty minutes before bed to settle down naturally. If the online access you have is introducing you to content that isn't healthy, put some restrictions in place to protect your heart and mind.

And truly, as today's verse says, keep your eyes on Jesus and focus on what He is doing in your life and around you. That's far more exciting and helpful than locking your eyes to a screen all the time.

1) Is technology becoming an unhealthy distraction in your life? In what ways?
2) What are some changes that you can make?
3) What benefits do you see to tech?
4) What negatives do you see to tech?
5) Are there any other changes you can make to balance the tech in your life a bit better?

PRAYER Father, I appreciate how technology has made some things easier in life and provides some good things. But I also see how it can hurt, and I want to be careful of that in my life. Please help me to be wise about my tech use and find ways to balance it. I need Your help to be a good steward of the technology in my life. It's in Your name I pray. Amen.

WEEK 48 The Pros and Cons of Social Media

So, whether you eat or drink, or whatever you do, do all to the glory of God.

1 CORINTHIANS 10:31 (ESV)

Social media can be fun, and it's a great way to stay in touch with friends and family all over the world. We can even make new friends on it. You know, a lot of the friends I have today I first met on Instagram.

On the flip side, social media can be dangerous. A friend of mine is a Christian therapist who works mostly with children and teenagers. Many of the people she sees have issues that come from social media use. The bullying, comparing oneself to others, and access to unhealthy things can make people feel sad and alone.

As with technology or anything that starts off fun, like sports or hobbies, you must be careful of the influence it can have in your life. If you're consumed with social media, you can start to shape your identity and measure your worth based on the number of likes and followers you get. You might begin to spend less time talking to the people right in front of you and instead be focused on commenting on a post by a stranger who lives halfway around the world.

I'm an adult and I still find myself getting sad sometimes when I scroll through my Instagram feed. I see other women who are beautiful or successful, and I start to compare myself. I get depressed. And all because of a few minutes on Instagram.

Is this how you feel sometimes? It stinks, doesn't it? And it can be hard to snap out of. Which is why we should be careful about how much time we spend and who we interact with on social media.

Don't let social media become a trap. If you start feeling distracted, unworthy, or sad, take a break. God has far more for you to enjoy and be a part of outside of social media.

When you do spend time on social media, do it for His glory. Use it to tell others about God and how good He is!

1) Do you ever find yourself feeling bad after looking at social media? How do you usually feel and react?

2) How does social media affect your worth or value?

3) Are there some limits you think you might need to set to keep yourself healthy and focused on God, family, and school? What are those limits?

4) Make your own list of social media pros and cons.

5) How can you use social media for His glory?

PRAYER God, thank You for social media's ability to keep me connected to my family and friends! But sometimes social media can leave me feeling discouraged or sad. Will You please help me to use (and not use) social media in a healthy way? Please, Lord, give me wisdom for my social media use. Thank You. Amen.

WEEK 49 The Comparison Trap

When I was in junior high, there was this girl everyone liked. She was popular, pretty, and nice (which is rare, am I right?). Her name was Mandy, and I wanted to be like her. I wanted to be liked by everyone, just as she was.

But I wasn't Mandy, and instead of trying to figure out who I truly was, I spent my energy and time trying to be her, someone who I wasn't. Because I didn't focus on being the best version of myself in junior high, this attitude carried into high school. It took me years to become comfortable in my own skin.

Comparison is one of those things we all face, usually pretty often. Social media doesn't help. We see other girls showing the best parts of their life, often leading us to believe their life is great and ours isn't and sending us into a pit of discouragement.

The truth is, no one has a perfect life, and we all hurt at times. Comparing someone's life to your own is like trying to fit together two completely different puzzle pieces that don't match.

God has given you a lane to run in, full of purpose and passions and plans! He has something very specific for you to do. If you're

So since we find ourselves fashioned into all these excellently formed and marvelously functioning parts in Christ's body, let's just go ahead and be what we were made to be, without enviously or pridefully comparing ourselves with each other, or trying to be something we aren't.

ROMANS 12:5–6 (MSG)

trying to cross over into another lane, you'll go unfulfilled in your own walk with God and destiny.

Instead of investing your time and energy into being like someone else, find out who you are! If you find yourself comparing your life with that of another, pray and ask God to give you focus on your own life. Start giving your time and attention to what God has put in your life.

There is enough for all of us in God's Kingdom. Another's win isn't a loss for you. God is big enough, and there is enough to do for you and everyone else to make a difference!

1) Do you find yourself comparing your life to someone else's?

2) What are you envious of, and why?

3) What can you do today to stop focusing on their life and start focusing on God?

4) Think of all the gifts in your life. What are you most thankful for?

5) How can you start using some of the things God has given you for His Kingdom?

PRAYER Jesus, You are perfect in every way, and I'm so grateful for You and how You created me. Sometimes I find myself comparing my life with others', turning envious and becoming discouraged. I don't want to live this way. I want to be grateful for the blessings in my life and live in the fullness of who You have made me to be. Will You please help me to fight comparison and be who You created me to be, with complete dedication to You? Thank You, Lord. Amen.

WEEK 50 Doing Your Creative Best

We talked about comparison and how harmful it can be. But I want to dig a little deeper into your purpose. This passage in Galatians is so helpful for fighting comparison and focusing on your own calling.

You might be wondering what you were created to do, what purpose your life has. I can tell you that you'll find those answers in God. You see, if you want insight into your design, you go to the Designer. And if you are worried about your future, you go to the One who knows the future.

Galatians 6 encourages God's people to make a careful exploration of who they are and what they are called to do. This doesn't happen passively or by accident—you must be intentional. You must seek it out. Knowing who you are and what you're meant to do is found only by leaning into Jesus and seeking His plans. When you find that out, commit to that journey.

Also, discovering who you are goes back to comparison. God desires you to stop looking at other people's lives and to focus on your own because He knows how harmful focusing on others is for your growth and transformation.

> Make a careful exploration of who you are and the work you have been given, and then sink yourself into that. Don't be impressed with yourself. Don't compare yourself with others. Each of you must take responsibility for doing the creative best you can with your own life.
>
> **GALATIANS 6:4–5 (MSG)**

Explore what God has for you and give your all to His plan. Do your creative best! I love today's verse and think about it often. *God, I want to give my creative best to everything You have for me.* I pray the same for you, dear. That you would sink yourself into God's plan for your life and give your all to that plan, for the good of others and His glory!

1) What are some things you enjoy or are passionate about doing?
2) What are some talents and gifts that you have?
3) How can you do your creative best in these areas and use them for God's glory?
4) How has comparison held you back from giving your all to something?
5) Is there anything you need to get rid of from your life in order to give yourself more fully to God's plan?

PRAYER Father, thank You for the gifts and talents You have put inside of me. I'm sorry I've strayed from Your design for me by comparing myself and trying to be like others. Will You please help me to keep my eyes on You and on the lane You have put me in? Show me what You want me to do, God. I want to do Your will! Amen.

WEEK 51 Vulnerability in a Fake World

I receive joy when I am weak. I receive joy when people talk against me and make it hard for me and try to hurt me and make trouble for me. I receive joy when all these things come to me because of Christ. For when I am weak, then I am strong.

2 CORINTHIANS 12:10 (NLV)

When I was your age, I always felt like I wasn't good enough. I picked this idea up from what people said about me or to me, and I started to believe them. I took their words and used them to determine my value. This even carried into my adult years and is something I still struggle with sometimes.

I remember one day I was feeling low, and God spoke to my heart these words: "What if you aren't good enough?" It blew me away! So many times I've heard Christians say, "You are good enough," so this idea from God sounded so weird. But then I opened up the Bible to 2 Corinthians 12, and there I began to understand the truth.

You and I aren't good enough in our own self and strength, that's true. But when we choose to lean into those parts of our lives that feel weak, we get access to God's strength!

It's hard to admit weaknesses or be vulnerable. In fact, it's flat-out scary sometimes. It makes perfect sense why you wouldn't want to admit weakness. This admission can make you feel like you aren't strong or capable enough, thereby making yourself vulnerable to people who can then hurt you.

For as long as I held back and closed myself off, I'm grateful that God helped me to open up to Him and to others. Because only when we lean into our weaknesses can we find His strength. And when we open up to others, we find love and support.

The Enemy would very much like for you to close yourself off from the world and for you to exhaust yourself by trying to be great. He knows that in exhaustion you are alone and tired, and he can get a foothold in your life.

Don't give him that opportunity. Open up your life to God and to others! Acknowledge your weak areas and invite God in to help you. Where you struggle to be vulnerable, talk to others. There is so much support out there for you—you don't have to do life alone!

1) Is there a weakness or an area you feel insecure in that you can turn over to God?

2) What are you holding back, trying to work out yourself, that you can share with God and others?

3) Who can you talk to about your struggles?

4) What seems scary about being vulnerable, and why?

5) What about God and Who He is brings you comfort and safety?

PRAYER Dear God, I feel unworthy and weak sometimes, and it makes me want to withdraw to protect myself. Or work really hard to prove to myself and to others that I can do hard things. But I don't want to lean on myself, Lord. I want to lean on You! Please help me to trust my weaknesses to You and be open with my heart and my life. In Jesus' name I pray. Amen.

Making a Difference

This is our last devotion together, and I am truly grateful for this journey we have been able to share. I suppose if there is inspiration I want to leave you with, it's for you to know how valuable you are in God's eyes. You're not here by accident, and He does have a plan for your life.

And you don't have to do this journey on your own. God wants to take the journey with you and lead you into the harvest.

It starts with trusting Him with *all* your heart! You might attempt to figure out some things on your own or desire to try to do things with your own strength alone, but that's where failure happens. Remember, leaning into your weaknesses gives you God's strength!

Sweet girl, trust God and give yourself to knowing Him as much as possible. There is no better way to spend your time than by getting to know Him. The more you know Him, the more you'll love Him. From that love, so many amazing gifts will overflow into your life. Your relationships, academics, emotions, and future will all feel brighter and more purposeful in huge ways.

If you will trust God and seek to know Him, you will find your paths made straight, meaning God will take care of you on your journey.

You will never regret getting to know God and spending time with Him. This world and everything in it will one day disappear, but God will stand true forever. Invest in your future with the daily desire of knowing Him.

He will in turn use you to accomplish splendid and wonderful things you never imagined you would get to be a part of! God has a purpose for you, and it's to make a difference on this earth for His glory.

1) How has this book inspired you most?

2) What distractions has it revealed to you that keep you from running more fully after Him?

3) How have you been relying on your own understanding, and how will you turn that over to trusting God?

4) Have you been given an insight into how God might like to use you?

5) Share a prayer for how you would like to step forward from this book.

PRAYER Heavenly Father, thank You for always having a plan. Nothing happens that You don't already know about, and You can definitely take care of me. As I move on from this book, please help me to remember what You have taught me. I want to go forward changed. More trusting of You and secure in our relationship. Giving every part of my life to know and follow You. Thank You for this journey, and please, keep me as Yours. Use me for Your glory, Lord, and to help others know You! Amen.

Acknowledgments

I'm so grateful to be chosen by God and have the opportunity to live for Him each and every day. I'm constantly amazed that He saw my wrecked sixteen-year-old heart and saved me anyway. And I'm beyond grateful to be used by Him to write this book for His daughters. God sees us and He hears us, girls—He is always faithful and trustworthy.

I'd like to acknowledge a few very important people who helped me to get here.

To my own mentors who took me in as a baby Christian in my late teens: Casey Gibbons, Sarah Blankenship, Deb Cook, and Debbie Lindell, all pastors' wives at my church who spent hours and years pouring into my life. I would not be who I am today without your investment.

To my nieces, whom I had in my heart when I wrote this book. You are some of my favorite people, and I pray for you all often, asking God to draw you near to Him and show you His loving kindness in the most beautiful ways possible. God loves each of you more than you'll ever know.

And finally, to Abigail See. Thank you for opening up your heart to me in this process and helping me to navigate what girls your age are going through. This book is better because of your investment and honesty. Thank you, sweet Abby.

About the Author

BRITTANY RUST is a writer and Bible teacher with a passion to help women know God and His Word. She is the founder and president of Truth x Grace Ministries, which provides online ministry for moms, events for women in Colorado, and online resources to help people grow in their faith.

Brittany is married and a mom to two. She enjoys a good outdoor adventure, Andy's Frozen Custard, nibbling on her son's yummy cheeks, and binge-watching period dramas. She and her family live in Colorado.

Parents, for more information on the author, follow her on social at:

Instagram: @brittanyrust

Facebook: /brittanyrustofficial

Twitter: @brittany_rust